PRAISE FOR

Rare and Used

Adventures of a Book Scout's Apprentice

"If this book were a store, you could count on finding treasured books inside. If it were a guide to a career sweetly oblique from greed, you could learn the ropes for simple happiness. If it were the profile of a friendship with an eccentric book saint, you could savor the company of this winsome character. If it were a quest for one's own quirks and loyalties, you could interrogate your own. Happily, *Rare and Used* is all these things in one. It's a compelling read for lovers of bookstores, books, and the people who haunt them. Every story, every paragraph delivers timeless lore from the book trade, with impish affection."

—Kim Stafford, author of *As the Sky Begins to Change*

"Daniel Dietz's narrative takes the reader through the winding stacks of used bookstores, church sales, and book fairs in the Pacific Northwest to share the buzzy highs and stomach-dropping lows of the book scout's ultimate quest: finding what you seek and eking out a living amidst it. Exploring the bonds of family, apprenticeship, and friendship, with homages to the complex and still under-examined works of Diane di Prima and Joanne Kyger, this story grapples with the constant flow of books in and out of the lives of those who love them."

—Mary Catherine Kinniburgh, co-owner of Granary Books and author of *Wild Intelligence: Poets' Libraries and the Politics of Knowledge in Postwar American*

"I had to keep looking over my shoulder while reading this book; I know the world of it so deeply I felt spied on. I too was raised between stacks of mildewing, hoarded, treasured countercultural books with penciled prices inside. I too island-hopped up and down I-5 between crusty used bookstores that might contain a newly unboxed Snyder, Kyger, di Prima, Sund, Han Shan, etc. I know the hunger. Also, like Daniel, I have aged into knowing the futility of trying to hold on to anything, that the visionary transcendence of the poem doesn't live in the paper it's printed on. He writes with such tenderness and humor about this very specific path, deeply attached to poems of nonattachment, clothing smeared with mustard. What actually matters? We keep seeking, each in our own insane way."

—Phil Elverum, songwriter, musician, and producer

Rare and Used

ADVENTURES OF A BOOK SCOUT'S APPRENTICE

Daniel Dietz

Oregon State University Press Corvallis

Oregon State University Press in Corvallis, Oregon, is located within the traditional homelands of the Marys River or Ampinefu Band of Kalapuya. Following the Willamette Valley Treaty of 1855, Kalapuya people were forcibly removed to reservations in Western Oregon. Today, living descendants of these people are a part of the Confederated Tribes of Grand Ronde Community of Oregon (grandronde.org) and the Confederated Tribes of Siletz Indians (ctsi.nsn.us).

Cataloging-in-Publication data is available through the Library of Congress.
LCCN 2026013220

ISBN 978-1-962645-74-4 paper; ISBN 978-1-962645-75-1 ebook

♾ This paper meets the requirements of ANSI/NISO Z39.48-1992 (Permanence of Paper).

First published in 2026 by Oregon State University Press
Printed in the United States of America

Oregon State University Press
121 The Valley Library
Corvallis OR 97331-4501
541-737-3166 • fax 541-737-3170
www.osupress.oregonstate.edu

for A, B, C, and D & M

Contents

CHAPTER ONE

The Rose City Book & Paper Fair

When Michael Karn invited me to join him at the Rose City Book & Paper Fair, I had roughly half a lifetime's worth of reasons to decline. As Michael's stepson, I had grown up among the characters who made their living picking books at thrift stores to resell at book fairs, or at thin margins to brick-and-mortar bookstores. I still had books that Michael had passed on to me when I was small—about movie monsters and cricket and whatever else he couldn't resell. After decades away from the book trade, I had a decent job, a receding hairline, and kids of my own. I didn't need Michael's books.

But Michael needed me. The book fair, where serious booksellers offered their most rare and valuable books, was up in Portland. To make the two-hour trip from his home in Eugene, Michael needed my air-conditioned Prius, or else he'd have to drive his old beater with the windows down, letting the June pollen in and causing him to sneeze and shout, "Yee-how!" In desperation, he would wipe his nose on the sleeve of his suit coat, risking further degradation to his appearance and to his reputation among fellow booksellers—if they noticed these things. I wondered if they would remember Michael.

I drove across town to find Michael waiting on the porch of his sagging house in Eugene's Whiteaker neighborhood. The brew pubs and restaurants that had once drawn visitors and money to the neighborhood had started to close, leaving residents to stew in their gonzo vibes, under pirate flags. Michael sat next to the stack of cardboard boxes that he used to scoop up books from library sales and then to resell in town, with mixed results, to the Smith Family Bookstore.

For our trip, Michael had chosen the suit jacket that my mom had compelled him to buy for my graduation from high school, twenty-five years earlier. After decades of dubious meals, Michael had qualified under Medicare for a weight-management medication, meaning that the jacket now drooped from his boxy shoulders, sagging open where his paunch had been. He paired the jacket with hiking pants, the kind with the option to unzip down to shorts. He completed the look with a Seattle Mariners cap so grimy that you'd have thought he was superstitious. He wasn't. Finally, Michael held the cane that—my mom had reminded me—he began using as an accessory when he was thirty but that he now needed.

"Looking sharp," I said.

Michael ran his skinny fingers over his mustache. "Want coffee?" he asked.

"No, thanks," I said. "I don't want to spill it in the car." I'm not fussy, but he would, I knew, carry his mug in the car with no lid. If Michael had a particular scent, old coffee was part of it.

"Okay, no coffee for you," he said. "Hold on while I get some."

I watched Michael shuffle back inside. If you're not put off by the loose, gray strands of hair falling from the sides of his gleaming pate, the droopy mustache under his prominent nose, or the mustard on his sleeves, Michael and his piercing blue eyes were unexpectedly handsome. He was tall and distinctive. Though I didn't have Michael's DNA, I had his blue eyes and now, his gray hair, so that people assumed I was his son. My frame was smaller, rounded out by midnight ice cream during my children's first years. To answer Michael's mustache, I grew a short beard. The shyness I'd inherited from Michael, the pleading quality in our blue eyes, reaffirmed our resemblance.

Michael was quiet and deferential, the kind of person you could talk to on the phone for hours, if you had plenty to say. Among our few family friends was a Canadian book scout who would call every week to talk about the used-book situation in British Columbia. After he died, without missing a week, the scout's widow started calling Michael. At first, she would tell him about her grief, then about her deceased husband's books, and finally about the price of produce at the grocery store. Michael listened with patience to all of it.

Michael suffered beneath his calm exterior from a pathological level of indecisiveness. He'd spend an hour with a diner menu, weighing the potential for regret if he ordered the Reuben instead of a basic pastrami on rye. This anxiety could be debilitating. He would never leave home without moving from room to room and performing a loud refrain, "OFF, OFF, OFF," as he obsessively checked each appliance. Or if he had to park on a public street, he would adjust his truck backward and forward—and then spend the rest of the day wondering whether a bumper might be hanging an inch over into the yellow. He never got a single parking ticket, but the cost to his inner peace was staggering.

This combination of calm and anxiety defined Michael as both a person and a book scout. Michael never sought out books by specific authors about particular subjects. He let books come to him, and when something of value washed up, Michael vacillated his way into a deep anxiety about whether to keep it or sell it. If he sold a valuable book, he regretted it. If he kept it, he stewed over the chances he'd missed to sell it. This pattern matched a personal life in which Michael was married to every woman he dated, for a time, and loved each of his children fiercely, though in varying degrees of proximity.

Growing up, I rode shotgun in Michael's red Toyota pickup from the thrift stores across the Willamette Valley up to the buying counter at Powell's Books in Portland. He kept scraps of food in his pocket or stashed away in his truck—a piece of bread, a packet of mayonnaise—so that an improvised meal was always at the ready. I took for granted that the way he worked was different from most folks, and that I was always part of it. I manned the radio dial, and since the truck didn't have AC, we kept the windows down and sneezed out the pollen, "Yee-how!"

After Michael settled into the Prius with his open mug, I began, with his help, to recall the world of book dealers we'd known back in the 1990s. We tried to recall the names of the booksellers, an old married couple, who had also run a small school from their house by the Luckiamute River, between Monmouth and Corvallis. They were called, we guessed, either the Trumans or the Prices, and even back then they seemed older than the sun. They looked like they had stepped out of a Woody Guthrie song, forthright and earnest, unlike any other sellers you might meet at a fair. They specialized in antique children's books, of course.

Michael and I arrived at our destination, a showroom in a hotel complex that had been built to serve the hollowed-out Lloyd Center Mall. Oak trees cast long shadows over what little activity took place outside. The parking meters had all been sabotaged, spray painted, so the parking was free.

As Michael shuffled forward, my heart raced the way it had at book fairs in my childhood, that old mixture of excitement and fear rising in my throat.

"You feel ready?" I asked. As a grown-up, I wanted to be able to talk about how we were feeling.

"Ready for what?" he said. "Nobody has good books anymore."

"Wait, so why did we come to Portland?" I asked.

"Just to remind us."

Walking ahead of Michael, I wondered whether he really felt any less urgency to get to the books. I doubted it.

After I paid our $5 per-person entrance fee, Michael stepped into the fair looking like a formerly distinguished Seattle Mariners fan ready for an impromptu hike. I followed him in, and the air of stale books and people dissolved my decades away. I was right back where I'd started on my journey toward adulthood, following Michael through crowds of people browsing display tables covered with books. The handwritten notecards next to the books in glass cases had staggering prices—$5,000, $10,000. And then I remembered: whatever you think a book is worth, you need someone willing to spend the money to buy it.

Regaining my bearings, I started to see the fair differently, for what it was: about forty different booths, each approximately a hundred square feet, with a few hundred books displayed on cheap, foldable shelves. The glass cases were uniform, rented from the hotel. The smell of old books was accompanied by a tinge of hotel linen from the draped tables. From a perceptible grade in the floor, I could tell that the venue had once been a parking garage, dressed up with windows and carpeting. The fair was literally off kilter.

The crowd moved with quiet intensity, book people murmuring to each other about price and condition, careful to avoid saying what they really wanted or how much they might pay. Hanging around each booth was a book dealer or two, someone like Michael, maybe a few years younger. Michael matched his surroundings so well that even at a few feet's distance, I worried that I might lose him. He'd studied the map of vendors in the car and was now using his cane to beat a path directly to Studio Books, a booth belonging to Gerry Rouff.

As we approached Gerry's booth, I recognized him instantly and recalled how he would turn up wherever I used to follow Michael. Gerry stood out among book dealers with his friendly, open presence. He loved talking about writers and artists and their movements, but it never felt like snobbery. He made people around him feel like they had something to add to any conversation. He cared more about the contents of his books than their value. Though he was Michael's age, Gerry's full head of tousled gray hair always made him look younger. His clothes were clean and unremarkable and gave the impression that he could've had a regular job. He had the small features and cheerfulness of a pet terrier that happened to be trained to find obscure art books. He appeared untroubled wherever he went.

Michael and Gerry exchanged only lukewarm greetings, despite having known each other for thirty years. Michael probed Gerry for details about his sales, and with little resistance Gerry revealed that he'd sold an expensive book to another dealer in the first hours, recouping the cost of his booth. The formalities dispatched, we turned to Gerry's books, all of which were interesting in one way or another but not indispensable to a collection. There was a handsome printing of one of Elizabeth Bishop's lesser works. There were three or four hardback first editions of the glut of B. Traven novels published in the wake of *Treasure of the Sierra Madre.*

Though decades had passed since Gerry and I had last talked, our conversation resumed where it had left off.

"Are you still collecting Burroughs?" he asked, meaning William S. and not Edgar Rice, whose books would have been the better investment. As a teenager I'd become obsessed with the Beat Generation, drawn to liberal depictions of substance use and sex. I learned more about life from the Beats than in any of my high-school health classes, though the lessons weren't exactly cautionary.

"No," I told Gerry. "I mean, I still have a couple of firsts somewhere—*Nova Express*, I think."

"It's not worth anything," Gerry said. I had forgotten I owned the book and still, I felt annoyed by Gerry's indelicate assessment. "Not unless you have *Naked Lunch*," he added.

"I don't."

I had been thinking that I might buy something from Gerry as a gesture, a nod to the unlikely friendship we'd once had, now revisited. I spotted a hardback collection of Kenneth Patchen's poems on Gerry's table and flipped through its pages.

"It's not worth anything," Gerry said, this time about his own book, which I was attempting to purchase. Before I could reach for my wallet, Michael rapped my leg with his cane, directing me into the neighboring booth.

Next to Gerry's Studio Books was Burnside Rare Books, the vendor who had bought Gerry's most expensive book earlier that morning. The Burnside model, I inferred, was to buy up all the best books and then sell them at higher prices. They did so at a double booth with a rented glass case. I had only begun to peer into the case when an eager bookseller in a bright-yellow dress engaged me.

"We're Burnside Rare Books," she said.

I nodded in agreement, since this fact was consistent with the booth's signage.

"We specialize in twentieth-century first editions," she said. "Many of these are signed."

"Signed," I repeated. "That must make them more valuable," I added, under my breath.

Then I caught myself. I remembered how my mom had never really mixed with Michael's milieu of insecure, male booksellers. After I'd gotten away, I'd noticed that some of the thinking that I'd been wired with was faulty. I looked more closely at the booth's books—early first editions by canonical authors, often inscribed to other writers of note. They were worthy of their price and confident presentation. I was intrigued by this way of doing business that hadn't existed when I was growing up.

"Let me know if I can help with anything," the dealer added. "Would you like a catalog?"

I'd been staring at the stack of glossy pink-and-purple catalogs atop the glass case. They looked like art from the future—like they didn't belong at the book fair. I found the design ungainly at first, but the closer I looked, the more I wanted it. I accepted the catalog and followed Michael as he searched for an old friend, David Morrison.

David Morrison was not hard to find. He stood at his booth with the same raven-black hair he'd had in the 1990s, now dyed, I suspected. His eyes darted around, and he spoke urgently at people who paused to look at his books. I recalled that David was a conspiracy theorist who'd once fired Michael from a part-time job at his bookstore after Michael had described one of David's theories as kooky. Yet they remained on good terms.

Now, at David's booth, the first thing you notice is not a book but a prominent sign forbidding the use of cellphones. As someone who is skeptical of screen time and social media, I supported this position. But for David Morrison, it wasn't only about screen time—there was also the issue of the havoc caused by cellphones on the human brain. David had printed flyers on this and other important revelations to share with his customers at the fair. There were several books he might point you to, some of which happened to be for sale.

For Michael, as good a listener as you'll find, David Morrison was the perfect companion. They discovered that they both have grandchildren, and that they shared the concern about screen time. David had with him a paperback on the topic—titled *Glow Kids*—which he gave to Michael as a gift, for his edification. Michael reminded David how, when I was a teenager, we'd bought from him a book of Allen Ginsberg's photographs. Michael said we still had it somewhere, though he couldn't remember where.

David looked at us with something like wistfulness in his conspiracy-tortured eyes, perhaps yearning for the world before cell phones. I noticed that his collection had become more specialized—his impressive display of art and photography books winnowed down to a few curated shelves of books about government cover-ups and illicit drugs.

From David's booth, Michael retreated to the back corner of the showroom and found a chair. He gave me his blessing to continue browsing without him. I worried that I might buy something worthless without Michael's supervision, but since he could no longer ambulate, it was my only option. I would have to do it on my own.

I stopped at the glass case belonging to Chaparral Books, whose books, though less rare than Burnside's, had interested me. Inside the case was a crisp copy of the December 1947 magazine published by the Mazamas, Portland's mountaineering society, of which Gary Snyder had been a part. The cover was rustic blue card stock, the title printed in an old newspaper font. It made the magazine look older than it was, and it was Michael's age already. When I asked, I was told that this issue included Snyder's essay, believed to be his first published work, and that it was available for $200. The clerk offered to remove it from the case so I could inspect it, but I declined. I felt no desire then to possess it.

Working my way deeper into the sale, I saw something curious inside the glass case of a dealer I didn't recognize, apparently down from Seattle. A tall, thick stack of yellowing papers, bound seemingly by hand, it was a facsimile copy of every issue of the *Floating Bear,* the newsletter published across the 1960s by Amiri Baraka (who published as LeRoi Jones until 1965) and the poet Diane di Prima. I'd read about the *Floating Bear* back when I was a teenager, but I'd never seen an actual copy. While Baraka eventually found his audience, di Prima's work remained obscure—despite, as I recalled, the seductive liberation of her verses.

The collection before me was priced at $175, which was roughly the amount I deposited each month into my children's college savings accounts. It would fill the tank of my Prius six times, enough to get me to work and back for two months. Even as I walked away, I felt drawn to it. I'd once loved di Prima, or at least the books of hers I gathered as a teenage boy who was vulnerable to the call of the salacious Beats. Some books in my collection had vanished over the years—sold, lost, or given away. I'd moved on, I believed, and yet, my stomach churned as I walked away from the glass case containing the *Floating Bear.*

At a booth called Passages Bookshop, younger Portlanders scooped up armfuls of books by James Baldwin and Mary Oliver, Seamus Heaney and Tomas Tranströmer. The booth felt unburdened from the need to show off the bookseller's high-end collection. I allowed myself to buy a trade copy of a book of essays by

Kim Stafford, *Having Everything Right*, for $4. The title spoke to the sense of order I'd hoped to achieve in my life. I tried not to think about di Prima.

At the corner of the showroom furthest from the entrance, I found Crooked House Books & Paper. This was the store run by Scott Givens, who had left a thriving store in Albany to come to Portland, and who, Gerry had told us, was now the person in charge of the book fair. The savvy that a person would need to sell books among Albany's fast-food restaurants and vape shops made Scott sound like something of a hero to Gerry. But there was restraint in Gerry's explanation of Scott's move to Portland. I could sense the contours of a compelling story. It tugged at my stomach, just like di Prima and the *Floating Bear*.

Adrift in my own thoughts, I found Michael sitting to the side of the sale and scowling at the Burnside Books catalog. He'd exhausted his interest in the fair. I suggested that we visit Gerry one more time to say goodbye, and Michael obliged. There, I figured I would buy at least the collection of Kenneth Patchen's poems, worthless as it may be. He'd priced it at $15—not so much that my children couldn't go to college. When we returned to Gerry's booth, however, it was gone. Between my reencounter with di Prima, my curiosity about Scott Givens, and now, the Patchen that got away, I felt a pang of unfulfillment familiar from my adolescence.

"What happened to the Patchen?" I asked.

"I couldn't believe someone wanted it," Gerry said.

He tried to interest me in a book about Marcel Duchamp's passion for chess. If this book was of interest to someone, it wasn't me. Instead, I chose a collection of poems and fiction by various writers about the small wooden boxes made by the artist Joseph Cornell, each with an image of a bird. Cornell's birds ranged from lifelike to more artistic renderings, some settled in nests and others surrounded by artifacts of human life. All the birds were neatly contained in their boxes. *A Convergence of Birds*, the book was called. I paid $20, and we said goodbye to Gerry and left the fair.

Back in the Prius on the way home, I asked Michael if he had any major complaints about the day.

"No," he said. "It was pretty much a perfect day."

"Pretty much?"

"Well, I wore my hearing aids, but I still couldn't hear everything. I guess it doesn't matter. Gerry says the same thing every time."

"What does he say?" I asked.

"He says I need to sell off my books."

"You probably do," I said, thinking of the leaning towers of books in Michael's living room, his bedroom, the bedroom's closet, the attic, and any other part of the house where a book might fit. This was the central question now in Michael's life: what to do with his books. I worried that they would become my problem.

"Why don't you see if one of the dealers wants to come over and make an offer?"

Silence settled in between us, with only the gentle hum of the Prius to dampen the tension I'd created—or, more precisely, that Gerry had introduced. Michael struggled now with the essential tasks of the trade: finding books at sales, listing them online, and shipping away to paying customers. He'd stopped selling at the fair. But if he sold off his books, what would be left of him? If he didn't, I would inherit the problem.

"Vultures," he said, punctuating the conversation.

Left to contemplate Michael and the fate of his books, I shut off the cruise control and allowed the Prius to accelerate at its will. This question had arrived more quickly than I'd expected. It wasn't exactly the question I had anticipated, either. Whatever happened to his books, I wondered about the meaning of my relationship with Michael—my stepfather, who had raised me—and then about the nature of possession itself. What does anyone actually get to keep?

CHAPTER 2

The Apprentice

I was five years old when Michael met my mom, Diane, at a party given by a professor who had gathered students from the margins of Fairhaven College, in Bellingham, Washington, to drink wine and complain about Ronald Reagan, then running for his second term. As the party stretched into the evening, Michael joined the conversation around the backyard bonfire, where Diane worked her way through a pack of True Blues and graduate students railed about supply-side economics. Diane had finished her degree and decided she would never rely on a man for money. Michael was working what would turn out to be his last real job, at the local food bank, where he was also a client. They planned a date, discovered that they both liked Tom Robbins and that neither cared much for society's norms and expectations, and became inseparable. I lived with my mom and became part of the experiment when these rarities converged.

Soon after I met Michael, we all moved in together to a drafty old house in downtown Bellingham, rented cheaply because the foundation was giving out. It was the first time my mom and I had moved in with someone else. Michael, who had been a bachelor, brought his scant personal effects, dozens of boxes of books, and a small dog that he called Puppy, who was at least twenty years old and either incontinent or never house-trained.

Puppy had remained in Michael's life when an ex figured he would take the breakup better if she left the dog. It's hard to imagine Michael dating someone, including my mom. If he were to have you over for dinner, you might be treated to his specialty, rice with butter, topped with cheese from the food bank. "Government cheese," Michael called it proudly. This spell worked on Diane, and we became a family.

I had my own room and was learning to sleep apart from my mom. In my bedroom sat a gift from Michael—perhaps because he couldn't resell it: a book on Alfred Hitchcock's films, filled with stills from *The Birds*. The book terrified me.

My mom left early in the morning for work, and so it fell to Michael, as we were becoming acquainted, to take me to school. I had just learned to tie my shoes and was still excited to be in charge of lacing up my red hightops before he rushed me out the door. Michael was always in a hurry to drop me off so that he could be the first scout inside the thrift stores when they opened. Once, as I slipped my foot inside a shoe, I felt the cold dampness of Puppy's excrement seeping into my sock. His dog had shat in my shoe, and I had put my foot in it.

"Goddamnit!" I shrieked. It was the worst word I was ready to say.

Michael, from another room, hollered back. "What?"

I kept shouting, dammit, dammit, my voice high and curdling. Eventually he was in the room with me, but he moved and spoke so goddamned slowly that I couldn't understand his words.

He was telling me to take the shoe off, and that's when I realized that my foot was still inside it. I saw white, blinded with the kind of rage that can only be known to a five-year-old whose foot was stuck in poop.

"Damnit," again. And then, "God fucking damnit."

And with that, I exhaled. I had broken a boundary, at least for myself if not my parents.

Michael laughed. "Sounds right," he said.

I calmed down enough to let him remove my foot from the shoe, and to peel off the wet, sticky sock.

Michael lifted me up and over his shoulder, sack-of-potatoes style, and carried me to the bathroom. He set me down on the edge of the tub and turned on the water, adjusting it to a temperature that was warm but not hot. He lathered soap onto his own hands and then brought my foot, gently, under the running water. Michael used his hands to scrape the mess off my foot, seemingly unbothered by the smell and its source. When he was done, he washed his own hands, then hoisted me back up into his arms, dried my foot, and set me on the floor.

"You did good," he said. "I'll have a talk with Puppy."

In this way, our days together vibrated with chaos and tenderness. My mom worked long hours, leaving Michael and me to our own devices. I joined him after school on thrift-store runs. He would pick me up in his old Dodge Dart, with a snack of government cheese cut into rough sticks, like French fries, with ketchup for dipping. I would eat my snack as we drove across town, and if the Dart didn't break down, we would check out the Salvation Army Thrift Store and the Humane Society's book nook.

When I was nine, Michael and Diane decided to marry. The vows and paperwork were handled at a psychic's house in downtown Seattle. If the psychic had any premonitions, she didn't share them, and her sense was that the Goddess was generally pleased with the union. For purposes of efficiency, Thanksgiving dinner at my grandma's house doubled as the reception, and we gorged ourselves on turkey and sparkling apple cider.

In Seattle, Kurt Cobain was smashing guitars, and back East, Bill Clinton played the saxophone. Meanwhile, my mom took a job down in Salem, where our family spent the 1990s marching to the beat of its own drum, to the rhythm of Michael's book scouting. On Tuesdays we'd visit The Arc for the yellow tag sale; Thursdays, the Humane Society Thrift Shop, where books were half off. Though we spent our time in thrift stores, our family story is not one of poverty.

In literature about working-class white families, there's often an instinct to make the struggle seem bleaker than it was. We occasionally ate food from the food bank, but we always had food. Whatever we may have lacked, we had enough books for this lifetime and the next. What made our family unique was not dire circumstances, but the eccentric choices my parents made with the resources we had.

By the time I was ten, Michael and I were recognized at every store in Salem. He would lead us in, his head and belly bobbing. Though I didn't have Michael's distinct nose or bulbous physique, I mirrored his furtive movements. We were a pair.

As Michael's apprentice, I was trained to spot value in the fiction section. My first lesson was humbling: no fiction is valuable. Which is why he left it to me.

To scout the fiction stacks, you build and maintain a mental checklist of writers—ones people like but whose books are scarce enough that you can sell them. On a successful trip you might find one or two books in the fiction section worth buying. A modern first edition would retail for $20, double that if signed. A first edition of a first novel published in a small run in the early or mid-twentieth century could be worth hundreds, maybe thousands, depending on the writer and the book. To find one is exceedingly rare. It's not a lucrative hunting ground for an experienced scout, who can find more value in nonfiction if he knows what he's doing, but it's a low-stakes training ground for an apprentice, as I was. You learn how to read publisher pages, to suss out book-club editions from first editions.

In the "A" section, you always look for Edward Abbey. A first edition of the *Monkey-Wrench Gang* increases in value with each rising degree in the Earth's temperature. On the "B" shelves, you might find James Baldwin, whose novels were first published as pulp fiction because of regrettable marketing mores of the mid-twentieth century. The genius of *Giovanni's Room* shines through.

At "C," you check books by Raymond Carver for overlooked inscriptions to one of the friends and neighbors around the Pacific Northwest who knew him. In "D," there's value in Didion, especially if you can find the rare fiction from her early career. Better known for her magazine essays, she moonlighted as Henry James if he grew up in a middle-class Sacramento enclave and smoked exactly five cigarettes a day.

Michael trained me to skip authors whose surnames begin with "E" and "F." You're not going to find a first edition of Fitzgerald in a thrift store. You can also move quickly from "G" through "I." Apologies to Ishiguro and the remainders of the day.

"J" produces occasional finds, but "K" can be lucrative, and not because of Jack Kerouac, whose books are fetishized by poorly trained scouts. You're looking for William Kittredge, who, like Carver, lived and worked in the Pacific Northwest, and whose spare, elemental prose keeps readers devoted.

The writer to look for in "L" is Ursula K. Le Guin. Though her popular science fiction was published in massive runs, her best writing traveled too close to reality for sci-fi readers and came in smaller printings. Her ideas continue to resonate in the changing world.

Be cautious in "M." Thrift stores are lousy with Frank McCourt's depressing books about Ireland. Readers can tell the difference between misery and merit.

Joyce Carol Oates is the name in "O," but she's written so many fine books that none of them are worth much.

You can pluck Michael Ondaatje's small press collections from the tessellations of Ralph Fiennes's face on now-a-major-motion-picture paperbacks of *The English Patient.*

In "P," there's a market for Pynchon among his neurotic readers—but the unwieldy novels are a pain to lug around.

If you find a first edition of Ayn Rand in "R," remember that eventually you'll have to deal with the kind of person who collects her books.

"S" is the exception where it pays to scout the American canon. You can tell by lifting a Steinbeck whether it was printed by a book club, and if not, even a second or third printing is valuable. Because his best-known books were printed in so many different editions, it is not impossible to find a genuine first edition of a classic Steinbeck novel.

Then there's Wallace Stegner, somehow less known. He did his best writing later in his career, and you can still find first editions, though they are seldom very valuable, in thrift stores.

Once you get to "T," do not go gently to the counter with a book by Dylan Thomas. His appetite for life would shock our twenty-first-century sensibilities, but it endeared him to a devoted contemporaneous readership. He's too common to be valuable.

"U" and "V" are useless except for Vonnegut.

"W" includes giants—Evelyn Waugh, Edith Wharton, and Oscar Wilde. But you can skip right past them and go straight for David Foster Wallace, who rants in the style of an encyclopedia, unbothered by the demands of storytelling, and who remains a legend among the literati of Instagram and TikTok.

While you're there, keep an eye out for Derek Walcott, the Caribbean poet and novelist whose reputation is burnished by Hilton Als's recent *New Yorker* essays.

Zoom through the rest of the alphabet and you're done, usually in less than five minutes if you know what you're doing. Most decisions then had stakes of 25 or 50 cents, now $1 or $2.

Looking at books this way left me with cynicism toward certain authors and their work, including beautifully written books that were published in large runs. A wry voice inside me would say that Stephen King was no good; now, it's Marilynne Robinson. All these years later, I still battle my instinct toward defensive irony. I'm trying to love what I love sincerely.

If you spend all day looking for scarcity in books, you start to look for it in people also. Maybe this is what Michael and Diane saw in each other that night in Bellingham, at the professor's party. Two rare editions, never before published, with immense appeal but only to the cultured reader who would appreciate their uniqueness. A man who knows every last detail about nearly every book published in the twentieth century, how and why the book came to be, and how much wealth an interested reader may be willing to part with. A woman with a college degree and a job, capable of paying rent and bills, and with a mouthy kid in need of steady care. It is in this way, it turns out, that I myself was plucked from the shelves of life and became part of Michael's collection.

❧

Beyond the daily grind of trips to thrift stores, Michael and Diane and I had our own ways of celebrating special occasions. Christmas, for example, was an exercise in moving books from one shelf to another. What happens is, you check the interests of friends and family against the books you found during the year at thrift stores and sales, minus those you've already resold. For Diane, Michael would search his piles for books about healthy cooking or a volume of poetry by an on-trend writer whom Diane had heard interviewed on public radio. Having bought several books that may be of interest to Diane in the course of his business, Michael would track them down in the nooks and shelves of the house, including among the boxes of books that Powell's and other stores had rejected, wrap them crudely, and place them under our family's Nutcracker.

For me, when I was little, Michael collected books about baseball, whether or not they were the kinds of titles that would interest a child. It may have been the Christmas after my eighth birthday when I got my first copy of *Ball Four*, Jim Bouton's memoir about the foul-mouthed amphetamine addicts of the Seattle Pilots during the 1969 season. Around that same time, I also got my first collection of Roger Angell's writing, much of it published originally in the *New Yorker*, an introduction to a world of ideas where before it was only balls and strikes.

I'd come into it each holiday dreaming of a Nintendo, a hope that faded when the gifts set out under the tree were flat and rarely thicker than an inch. And when we opened presents, revealing at last which books would transfer from Michael's collection to mine, it would take my developing brain a beat to place the subject of the book and to understand why it had been chosen for me. The three-volume set about the history of cricket in Australia wasn't something I'd asked for, and yet I was now the only person in our town, as Michael reminded me, with his own encyclopedia about baseball's Southern-Hemisphere cousin.

Unlike more-traditional families in which parents signify their affection for their children by showering them in material goods, our family honored the spirit of the exchange. If Michael had given me a book last year that I hadn't cared for—say, a picture book about monsters from movies that had given me nightmares—then I would have had no qualms about repackaging it and giving it to him the following year, matching the generosity of his initial thought and effort. Nor was he troubled by the return, since giving books back and forth, shuffling them around the house, was what he understood to be the purpose for the occasion.

Diane made her peace with this arrangement by decorating the house with mismatched lights and bringing out the oversized Nutcracker doll that was never really put away. Throughout the year it watched over us, lying sideways on the old glass case where Michael kept his best books. The wooden doll's tall hat and grim face were perpetually part of our family. For the holiday, the Nutcracker was set down on the floor and functioned as our family's tree, towering over the stacks of wrapped books.

After presents on Christmas Eve, we'd settle into the couch to watch the broadcast of *It's a Wonderful Life*, with the broken antenna on the television allowing waves of static to surge across the screen. I can see now how the story, for them, was so affirming, proving a corollary to Capra's notion: the peace one finds in giving everything away is also attainable by having nothing to begin with.

When *Wonderful Life* came on, I'd feel the natural surge of my body's melatonin wash over me and I would leave my parents in the living room, cozying on the couch with their faces warm and relaxed from our conviviality. From there, I'd retreat to my bedroom where the monster books lived, though I'd learned to hide them behind my bookshelf—not that I ever forgot about them.

I'd sit on my knees in front of my shelf and add my new books to my collection. My accumulation of baseball books was even more authoritative now that it included reference materials on its roots in cricket. For many of my books, the ones that were worth it, Michael had applied a Brodart, the mylar casing you find in upscale bookstores. Plenty of other kids had books, but none had books about cricket in Brodarts. I wasn't aware of any other third-graders who were into Roger Angell, either. Which is to say, I did not dwell on the Nintendo, and in its place, I received the philosophy that sustains every scout I've ever known: nobody has better books than I, which is why, even though I don't have any money, everyone else is an idiot. You may prefer Capra's more succinct title.

As I grew into adulthood, Michael's training clung to me like the smoke from my mom's True Blues, lingering no matter how hard I tried to scrub it off. I left home for good at seventeen and arrived at college confident that I already knew more, through books, than my classmates. At the same time, I was dogged by the suspicion that they belonged to the world in a way that I didn't have access to, that I could only glimpse from the outside. For the next two decades, I tried to hide the traces of my childhood by moving as far away as I could, cloaking myself in the status of a career, and binding myself to a partner who could watch *It's a Wonderful Life* without having an existential crisis. But as George Bailey learns when he loses everything, true wealth isn't money or status; it's the people who helped make you that matter.

CHAPTER 3

Sandwich Days

By the end of the twentieth century, Michael, like so much of the American experiment, had reached the height of his powers. Up and down the Willamette Valley, he knew where to find the best books and where to sell them. He could tell you the approximate value of any book he might see. Even physically, he was formidable—tall and skinny except for his round belly and a bulbous, balding head, making his body look like two cocktail onions speared together by a toothpick.

These were also my last days of searching for books with Michael. By the end of high school, I was ready to leave books behind for good and to go out into the world. I was young and fit and certain that I would find success. Nobody would mistake me by then for Michael's son. With one foot out the door, I agreed to join Michael at the Eugene Public Library book sale in April of that year, not knowing it would set in motion a chain of events that would haunt me twenty-five years later.

Michael guarded our position in line at the library sale with eyes that said, *take all the Stephen King you want but keep your hands off the hardback nonfiction.* He was desperate to fill a few boxes with books on natural history, fly-fishing, orchestral jazz. The subject didn't matter as long as he could resell it. If he found the right books, we would make it for another month.

Two kinds of people waited in line at six a.m. for the library sale to open. There were the readers—civilians who craved paperback mysteries and romances enough to set an alarm on a Saturday morning. And then there was this other kind of person, like Michael: usually male, oily hair, darting eyes, index finger extended and ready to pluck a book by its spine. You wouldn't describe this type as a bookseller, or even as a dealer. This unique specimen is called a book scout.

Book scouts once proliferated in proportion to the used books available to be resold profitably. In Oregon in the 1990s, to hear a book scout tell it now, there were signed first editions on every thrift-store shelf. It was the way you might expect an early settler in Oregon to describe the pristine Willamette Valley, where apples, they said, would grow to the size of your head. Pioneers chased this myth for a generation before the apples ran out, if they were ever there at all. In the glory days of scouting, rare books dangled from the branches, waiting to be plucked.

Just as wagons once descended on the open fields of the valley, new kinds of booksellers arrived and saturated the business. They flooded in through Amazon and eBay and left no box of books untouched. Volumes once left up in attics to grow in age and value were listed online by grandchildren with dial-up modems. The specialized knowledge earned by book scouts across years of desperate searching and stingy profits gave way to the Google search. Everyone with a computer became an amateur book scout. The real scouts became rarities.

❧

At the Willamette Valley's various library sales, which gave the scouting life its rhythm, Michael and I came to know the other scouts, who I realize now must have puzzled at us: Michael, scraggly and grand in his stained suit coat, trailed at every turn by a blonde kid who looked like he'd wandered out of a JCPenney ad. No less than Michael, I was a fixture at every sale, part of the scene.

When Michael spoke with other scouts, they mostly ignored me, unsure of how to engage with a child in the heat of the battle for all that is used and rare. Even among scouts, salutations were muted unless someone had a valuable find to brag about.

"Vito got a book on Alaskan expeditions with maps that fold out," Michael would lament when we were back in his truck.

"It might be a book club," I'd offer, referring to the cheap reprintings often mistaken for first editions. Michael and I were aligned in our belief that only he could pick the best and rarest books from any sale, and I felt pangs of regret whenever another scout beat him to a find. Though he never said as much, I came to believe that my role—to have Michael's back when he entered the fray—was indispensable.

❧

When volunteers finally opened the doors at nine, three hours after we had joined the line, a rush of adrenaline would jolt Michael's body into motion. He would advance on the books, unbothered if I fell behind.

Inside the exhibition hall of the Lane County Fairgrounds, the readers buzzed around tables of fiction like a veil of gnats. Michael cut through them to the table of books about the Pacific Northwest. He plucked anything of interest from the table and dropped it into a cardboard box, the first of many he would fill that day. Powell's would pay cash for *The Centennial History of Oregon*, say, or an early treatise on regional geology.

In the first minutes of the sale, Michael filled his boxes quickly from untouched sections, stashing his keep in a designated area to the side. Later, he would scrutinize each book closely, over against the wall, after scouring each section. Right now, it was about moving fast and getting to tables that had yet to be disturbed by the ravenous scouts.

You had to avoid the various sections of fiction planted like traps throughout the sale. Mystery, westerns, romance—even the titles that the library volunteers classified as "literature"—are genres with no value, I was trained to believe, except to the poor fools who read them. The volunteers paired sections together with incidental humor: self-help and car repair, US politics and animals. Michael cut through Nixon biographies and dog training guides, finally arriving at the table with books about music, his personal favorite.

Searching through thousands of titles is a lonely activity. Each scout is on an island with his own internal monologue and a century or two of humanity's triumphs and failures bound together in paper and cloth. In this context, finding a collection of Gary Giddins's essays on jazz was like running into an old friend. Michael preferred books to friendship, if the latter even existed among scouts.

Gerry Rouff would turn up wherever Michael went, though he seemed out of place to me when we found him at library sales. He was too dignified, too cheerful, to thrive in this environment. Gerry would hang around the art books, picking up one book at a time to study. He would keep the book only when he had conviction about its merits. You got the sense that he was always waiting for someone to come along to talk to.

"Hey, Michael. Find anything?"

"No." Michael wouldn't have told Gerry even if he had. "Did the vultures leave any art books for you?"

Gerry said something about Fluxus, and Michael began to walk away. One thing about Gerry is, even when he's talking to you, you can leave the conversation without goodbyes and pick the conversation back up at the next month's sale.

At sales like the one in Eugene, Michael might cross paths with the younger scout, Scott Givens, who was working then at a bookstore up in Albany. With no cardboard box, Scott lugged armfuls of century-old tracts on topics of obsolete interest. It would take him years to learn what was worth keeping.

Michael finished combing the tables and then hunched over his boxes against the wall, checking for inscriptions and underlining, and then sorting the books into piles to keep or discard. Once a scout has picked over the tables, he must decide which of the books he's gathered is worth keeping for a dollar or two, and which should be returned to the volunteers to place back on the tables.

Michael usually found disappointment on his second trip through the titles that had made it into his boxes, but at this sale he made a rare find. Out among the old hiking guides and natural histories, Michael had dropped into his cardboard box an early edition of *The Uttermost Part of the Earth*, by E. Lucas Bridges, who studied the tribes of the Tierra del Fuego at the very tip of the Southern Hemisphere. A volunteer had placed it in the Pacific Northwest section.

The edition that Michael found, upon closer inspection, was not the American reprint but was instead the first London pressing of the book. To Michael's delight, the book was in fine condition, almost fifty years after it was published, with no mark other than the author's signature. Michael estimated its worth at $1,000, meaning he could get $300 from Powell's. He might hold onto the book for a while if he didn't need the money right away. He would feel like the richest man in the Whiteaker, the neighborhood he called home in Eugene.

❧

Diane would have been happy enough if Michael never bought another book. She wrote for the local newspaper—not lucrative work, but it came with health insurance, and it provided a steady flow of not-quite-enough money to get by. She loved Michael dearly, but not necessarily for his aptitude with used books. Mostly she loved his patience, and how he was constantly, quietly present, going about his business and always coming home by mealtime.

Michael and Diane spent their days surrounded by books and unfinished projects in the living room of our sagging two-bedroom house. Through glasses perched on the edge of her nose, Diane attacked her projects with laser-like bursts of brilliance. To address the lack of access to feminine hygiene supplies for young women in Africa, Diane would sew reusable menstrual pads from noon to night—for months in a row. Then when gardening season came, she drifted from the sewing machine to the makeshift greenhouse she had installed at the center of the living room, with blinding grow lights. Before the plant starts were ready to go into the ground, she'd begin archiving her family photographs, leaving the plants to go to seed—still inside the house. She would pause the archiving project to send a greeting card to an old friend, months after the holiday in question, with language so precise that you wished she'd write a book. But she wasn't built for long-term projects. Her best efforts bloomed from wildly scattered seeds.

My mom was not an exacting partner for Michael. She'd grown up in a tidy home organized along the traditional lines of the nuclear family in the 1950s. Both her parents worked for Boeing, her father as an engineer and her mother as an executive assistant. They drove well-maintained cars and kept the lawn neat at their house in Seattle's eastside suburbs. After she left home, my mom searched for antidotes to the tedium of her upbringing, first travelling to Panama with the Navy and then marrying a logger. Finally, with me in tow, she settled into her skin as someone who gave her best effort of the day to her work and pursued hobbies—painting, sewing—with short bursts of zeal.

To the partnership with my mom, Michael, who'd grown up with hard-drinking parents and a wild pack of brothers in South Seattle, brought intrigue and culture, if not much income. In his best years he never made more than $1,000 a month. But he was resourceful, knowing where to find things for free, and unashamed to get his lunch at the community center when times were hard. Unlike his parents, Michael preferred books to bourbon. That's what would sustain him.

Michael may have cobbled together some semblance of his life without my mom, but her commitment to her career kept our family together and gave me possibilities beyond it. What my mom always understood, even if Michael didn't, was that you can't wait for everything to come to you. You have to hustle to get by. In their partnership, my mom provided Michael the spark of urgency he sometimes needed to get his business going. And she made sure he always had something to eat.

❧

When Michael came home from a book sale, Diane would be so engrossed in her latest passion—this month it was paint-by-numbers—that she would hardly notice him. She would be dropping thick globs of acrylic paint onto a numbered sequence across her printed outline of *Starry Night*. As the yellows and blues mixed, a greenish hue would emerge, giving the sky a sea-like quality and making the replication its own unique expression. Van Gogh would be mortified.

Michael always came home hungry from a scouting trip, but for him, it was only the beginning of the mission. After gathering stock from the library sale, he needed to get to Portland to sell the books for cash. But first, Michael would need a sandwich.

"Did you have anything for lunch?" he'd ask.

"Waiting for you, dear," she'd say. "I better eat something too."

"We still have some ham," he'd say. They always did.

"Yes, please."

"You want mustard on it?"

"Just mayo," she'd say, dabbing at the canvas.

"More mouse turds for me."

Michael would make a place amid the chaotic room for his boxes of books and, without washing his hands, would layer four slices of bread with a scoop of white mayonnaise, his with mustard in such a generous portion that it mingled and then coated the thick slices of ham and cheddar cheese that he placed on top of the bread. His sandwich dripped globs of mustard and mayonnaise, all of it swirled together with the chaotic brilliance of *Starry Night*.

CHAPTER 4

This Kind of Bird Flies Backward

In a submission to the December 1947 newsletter of the Mazama mountaineering club of Portland, Oregon, Gary Snyder wrote, "a man's first view of the mountains is like his first love; no matter how many there may be in his life, the first will never be forgotten." Snyder went on to become Kerouac's Japhy Ryder, leaping across boulders in *The Dharma Bums.* He published collections of poetry about the Himalayas and the mountains of Japan. One of them won a Pulitzer. Before all that, Snyder had declared with conviction as a seventeen-year-old that he would hold on to the mountain he loved first.

❧

My first love was a poet. And while Gary Snyder and other poets—Tranströmer and, most recently, Rena Priest—have become dear, my first, who will never be forgotten, is Diane di Prima. Less renowned than Snyder, di Prima lingers on the outer edges of the Beat canon. She was never memorialized in a Kerouac novel, nor did she fit in neatly with the male poets of the fifties who had grown up with a fair amount of privilege, lumped together as the Beat Generation. Di Prima's interests and career as a writer reached far beyond the bohemian tropes of the time. Born in Brooklyn to a family of Italian immigrants with roots in the communist movement of the 1930s, di Prima erupted onto the page, unbothered by the constraints of genre or convention.

She was beautiful. When di Prima published *This Kind of Bird Flies Backward* in 1958, she was twenty-four years old, with thick, red hair wrapping around her long face with its Roman nose, like a Modigliani painting rich with sophistication and intelligence. When she read her poetry, di Prima's voice was soft but adamant. She was new to the scene but she didn't care, and neither did her poems. She made you want more.

I was thirteen years old the first time I saw a photo of di Prima on the cover of a reprinted volume of *Memoirs of a Beatnik*. The book originally had been published as a pulp paperback, a collection of racy stories about the sexual exploits of beatniks. It was championed by Olympia Press, which had published *Lolita* and, later, the lurid works of William S. Burroughs and Henry Miller. When *Memoirs* was republished in the 1980s, intended to reach di Prima's more literary audience, the pulp cover was replaced with a photo of di Prima taken from around the time of *This Kind,* her early days as a poet. Sitting on an unmade bed, looking softly downward at her bare legs, di Prima was framed as a poet to fall in love with.

I discovered *Memoirs* as a teenager poking through the shelf of books that Michael kept for himself. Though he resold nearly everything, he kept bibliographies, price guides, and titles that tickled his fancy. Next to a volume of erotically illustrated bookplates, di Prima's book attracted me first with its title. Inside, she paired vivid descriptions of sex with mundane details of Beat life, like the dinner she would make by mixing mashed potatoes with ketchup, which she called menstrual pudding. The rawness of di Prima's scenes mapped onto my own burgeoning interest in the messy fecundity of the world around me. I became devoted to di Prima's work with an enthusiasm common to adolescent males.

Di Prima was my first lurid Beat writer, but others soon followed. I discovered Burroughs, whose *Naked Lunch* was mind-bending, but only if you hadn't found his other books. *The Ticket That Exploded*, with its descriptions of orgasms as "body-Magnetic silver flakes," sent pulses of electricity down and throughout the body. Indifferent to the queerness of Burroughs's writing, I was titillated by the abstractions, and also the not-so-abstract—the "bone wrenching spasm that popped silver light in our eyes."

This is not to say that I didn't also appreciate the quality of di Prima's work. Her talent cut through my hormones, speaking to me clearly in free form with revolutionary ideas. Her poems described bohemian scenes with irony and humor. From there, she veered toward mystical themes and back around to the political. In her "Revolutionary Letter #8," she wrote, "NO ONE WAY WORKS, it will take all of us/shoving at the thing from all sides/to bring it down." I didn't know what way she was talking about, or what we were shoving at. But I wanted to be part of it.

As Michael's protégé, I also was interested in the rarity and value of her books. I began to check the poetry section, searching for "D," whenever I entered a used bookstore. It was like looking in the hallway for your high-school crush; the less you saw her, the more you wanted to. On the other hand, W. S. Di Piero was everywhere. On those occasions when I found di Prima, it was usually *Dinners and Nightmares*, her second collection of poetry that got a generous run from Corinth. Once I had my copy, there was nothing exciting about finding another one. You might also find the City Lights edition of *Revolutionary Letters*, di Prima's more explicitly political work. While the first City Lights edition was valuable in good condition, you would usually find it covered in coffee stains, or with pages torn out.

The book I longed to discover for myself was her first: *This Kind of Bird Flies Backward*. I had no way of knowing what was in it, only that it had enough of her energy to force itself into the world. I also knew that it was rare, that I would be lucky to ever possess a copy. If I ever got one, I thought, I'd never let it go.

❧

After discovering di Prima, I would babble about her to Michael, without acknowledging the private moments I'd had with his copy of *Memoirs of a Beatnik.* He must have been excited by my enthusiasm for his trade, especially since I'd shown interest in tracking down different editions of her more obscure works. Michael received a catalog in the mail—before the internet, booksellers would send each other lists of their books on offer—listing a couple of signed, limited editions of di Prima's magnum opus, *Loba as Eve*, Parts I and II. I ordered them from the catalog—about $30 for each book—with the money I'd strung together buying and selling books alongside Michael. When the *Lobas* came in the mail, they were handmade and delicate, including a volume printed on paper made of onion skin, signed by di Prima. They felt so fragile and precious that instead of setting them out on the shelf in the room with the rest of my books, I kept them with Michael's rare books, in his glass case with our family's treasures, under the Nutcracker.

❧

In her actual memoir, *Recollections of my Life as a Woman*, di Prima recalls working on catalogs at the old Phoenix Book Shop in Greenwich Village to sustain her life as a poet. Book catalogs once served a key function: for more-obscure works to find their niche buyers. Booksellers around the country would print and send each other mimeographed catalogs in the mail. Buyers, who were often other booksellers, would then order books for potential customers or for themselves. This work employed a whole class of bookstore employees who remained behind the counter.

In my teenage years, some of the last before the internet was widely accessible, Michael shared his catalogs with me, noting books that I might find interesting. Though Michael never ordered anything, he read the catalogs he received carefully, downloading inferences about scarcity and pricing.

Before I was old enough to feel foolish, I decided to make a catalog of my books. My collection consisted mainly of beaten-up copies of Burroughs's books, the best of which was a hardback first edition of *The Wild Boys* that I'd bought from an old bookstore in Corvallis called Avocet. It had no dust jacket and was stained with coffee, but if it had been in decent condition, it would have been worth something.

I made the catalog in my typing class in high school, where, once we had exceeded a certain threshold of words per minute, we were left to entertain ourselves with the word processor. Though not an exemplary typist, I trained myself to hunt and peck fast enough to meet the threshold, and then proceeded to list my most valuable books, their conditions, and my estimate of their market value. When finished, I saved the document to a gigantic floppy disk, which I brought to Kinko's and used to print my catalog. I folded the printed pages, stapled them together, and brought the finished catalog home to show to Michael.

He was puzzled. "You made this?"

"Yeah, at school. Are the prices right?"

He read carefully. It wasn't a long document, maybe two letter-sized pages folded in half, no more than forty books in total. But it had taken me weeks to make, in addition to the sum total of the years I'd spent with Michael learning about the trade. I wanted his approval.

"You can't sell *The Wild Boys* for $180," he said. "It's not in 'Good' condition. You can list it as 'Fair.'" He handed the catalog back to me. "What are you going to do with this?"

I hadn't thought about it. The truth was that I had made it for Michael. I had only printed one copy. I didn't really want to sell my books, and even if I did, I wouldn't know how to run a mail-order operation.

"I'll show it to Gerry," he said, and with this, I felt like I'd made it. I liked Gerry, and back then, I looked up to him. He was friendly to Michael, and he knew every bookseller in the world, or at least in

Oregon. He also took time to talk to me, sharing whatever he knew about Beat poets. Gerry had worked at bookstores down in Berkeley long after the heyday of the Beats and the hippies, but not so long that he didn't occasionally have dealings with them and their books.

I wasn't around when Michael showed Gerry my catalog. I still had to go to school during the day. When I saw Gerry next, he was genuinely impressed. He referenced several of the books and offered to buy one, if it was still available. I hadn't expected this, and instead of arranging to sell the book to Gerry, I told him that someone else had bought it, an explanation that surprised us both.

❧

Looking back, I'm relieved that the catalog I made will be lost to time once Michael and Gerry are no longer around to recall it, if they haven't forgotten. My interest in the Beats embarrasses me; what passed for bohemian now seems so banal. Their early attempts at sexual freedom, in retrospect, reek of sexism. Di Prima describes how she was perceived, assumed to be an object of the men's liberated thinking, in *Recollections of my Life as a Woman*. I'm also aware that the substances the Beats used recklessly can ruin lives.

To make a family and work hard to keep it fed, housed, and thriving isn't the path of least resistance. It's one of the hardest things you can do. In my adolescent mind I reduced di Prima down to an object to collect. After reading her memoir, I see the full complexity of her life, the choices she made and the consequences. I see now how I turned her into a fantasy of Beat femininity rather than recognizing her as a poet and mother who held everything together. Di Prima created and endured much more life than could be held in the hands of a collector.

Michael never made a catalog of his books. He didn't go out of his way to amass books in any particular genre, nor did he form the kind of attachment that would motivate a dealer to memorialize his collection in this way. His approach was to let books come to him, when the price was right, and to let go of them, also when the price was right. Not to say that Michael didn't feel attached to some of his books, or that he didn't have affection for them. He just didn't let those things get in the way of his barely profitable business.

I wonder if Michael were to make a catalog now of his life—not just books, but with whatever mattered most to him—what would he list? What price would he assign? He had my mom and me, and I know he valued us because, when they were dating, he'd send my mom a $20 bill in the mail every now and again with no explanation. Later, Michael sold a book handmade by the poet Kenneth Patchen and used the profit to send me to summer camp. Through small and striking gestures, he would show people that he valued them.

Michael had two sons from relationships before we'd known him, one whom Michael had raised almost entirely on his own, and the other whom his mother had raised. I knew from how Michael talked about his sons that he loved them in a way that wasn't available to me, even as he cared for me and taught me his trade. Later in life, Michael connected with a daughter who hadn't been known to him. He was over the moon. The earnestness of Michael's loyalty to those he loves disarms any comparison.

There's also the matter of Michael having had multiple marriages, so that he was basically betrothed to everyone he ever dated. He loved each partner so fully that it would be absurd to wonder whether you were his first love or his fourth. If Michael's life were a catalog, it wouldn't feature a high concept like the one from Burnside Rare Books, or be full of expensive first editions. His list would include works of genius by lesser-known authors and obscure volumes of nonfiction that would be key to a definitive collection.

❧

Book catalogs would have disappeared except for a handful of dealers, including some in Oregon, who still produce them. Years later, I would discover catalogs from Burnside Rare Books so glossy and sleek that you could collect them. The prices on the books listed in those catalogs would surpass the annual earnings of most booksellers. Seeing these prices in catalogs, including for books that had passed through his possession, Michael griped about money he felt should be his. He didn't acknowledge that the high prices owed to the sophisticated catalogs that helped lure wealthy buyers, not from the books themselves.

I would later learn that Scott Givens, after he came to Crooked House Books & Paper, published catalogs with thoughtful descriptions of the cultural moment that produced each book. His 2024 catalog, "Hobos," includes an essay tracing listings back to the work of Nellie Bly and Jacob Riis, with care for context about people who slept outside then and now. Further back, Crooked House published a catalog focused on Victorian book bindings, emphasizing the work of the women—Sarah Wyman Whitman, Lee Thayer, and Margaret Armstrong—who were essential to their design within a male-dominated industry.

Some of the earlier Crooked House catalogs I found were credited to two booksellers, Scott Givens and Rachelle Markley. Though I knew of Scott through Michael and Gerry, I didn't recognize the other name. I remembered how Gerry had been opaque when he told us that Scott had taken over Crooked House, along with the duty of organizing the Rose City Book & Paper Fair. I looked for traces of this other bookseller in the catalogs, which were different from anything else I'd seen.

The most exotic catalog published by Crooked House was a cookbook whose dust jacket required the reader to cook it to make it legible. Additional catalogs were dedicated to writing by and for women. I wondered, with these beautifully formed collections, if Scott, like me, never actually intended to sell the books he collected in his catalogs. Or maybe it was his way of holding onto something rare, even as it got away.

❧

In his first published collection, Snyder wrote about riprap, the stream-worn pebbles cobbled into pathways through the mountains.

Snyder sees these pathways in language, with words placed solid, by hand, into rocky sure-foot trails.

By the time Snyder published *Mountains and Rivers Without End*, his epic poem written across four decades, it was a big enough deal that in his hometown, Portland, he could pack a venue to read his poems. And so, when the book came out in 1996, my family made a rare pilgrimage together to the Trinity Episcopal Church in Portland. After the reading, we assumed there would be a customary book signing. I chose something unique—not a book by Snyder, but the book of Allen Ginsberg's photographs that Michael and I had bought from David Morrison. In it, I'd found a picture of Gary Snyder carrying a birthday cake, per Ginsberg's caption, to his "difficult mother." She's turning eighty and, in the photo, she just looks tired.

Snyder smiled through his shaggy goatee when he saw the picture. "You know," he said, "it was di Prima who baked that cake."

"Diane di Prima," I said. Thinking quickly, I added, "What was she like?"

Snyder wrote his name carefully next to the photo and then looked up at me. "She was a tough chick," he said.

My turn was done.

Though it didn't surprise me to learn that the two poets' lives would intersect, I wonder now how Diane di Prima had come to bake a cake for Gary Snyder's mother. A cake takes time and patience. It takes work—a generous act. And yet, Snyder remembered di Prima for being "tough." Ginsberg remembered Snyder's mother as being "difficult." The rest of the photos in Ginsberg's book were of men, mainly the Beats, posing, projecting nonchalance but profoundly aware of their own beauty. Like teenage boys.

After growing up in Oregon, Gary Snyder had left for Japan and India, traveling for a time with fellow poet Joanne Kyger, whom he married. Later, Snyder would win the Pulitzer while Kyger's equally brilliant work remained known mainly to other poets.

As I prepared to leave home for college in Vermont, I started packing months in advance, shedding the detritus of my childhood—books, mainly—so that I would take with me only what was essential. I believed then that the complexity I'd known in my life could be pared down, smoothed over, and that by that process, I would succeed where my parents had stumbled. I didn't know then where I was headed or what I would need, only that it would look nothing like where I came from.

I stacked my books neatly into boxes, either to remain at the house or for Michael to sell so we could share the profits. Anything truly rare, like di Prima's *Lobas,* I tucked into the glass-encased shelf in the living room. I assumed that no matter how far I went, Michael and his books would always be back at the sagging house, waiting for me. I had the whole world ahead of me and no time left for Diane di Prima, my first love.

CHAPTER 5

Buyer Beware

After the library sale, Michael would need to convert his investment in books back to cash for his business to continue on. He never had more money than he needed to survive the coming days, so it was urgent that he complete the cycle.

The next step was to arrange a box of books to sell at Powell's, the largest used bookstore in the Pacific Northwest. Its buyer's table was the sun around which book scouts orbited, its light the cash they needed to keep going. It was also an exciting moment—to learn whether the judgment calls at the library sale would pay off. Nothing was guaranteed, though, so you had to choose books carefully and approach the buyer's table with a plan.

Michael sifted through the incongruous collection he'd brought home from the sale. There was a collection of books about primates. As he leafed through them, Michael adopted the internal monologue of a retired professor, an octogenarian leaving behind the core texts of his life's work. *What does the heart want?* Michael thought. It wants genetics, and it wants jazz. Genes and jazz, that's it. From his own collection, Michael added *Who's Who of Jazz,* a biography of Duke Ellington, and a book of Gary Giddins's essays on contemporary jazz. *Wait,* Michael paused. *The heart does not yearn for contemporary jazz. Nobody yearns for contemporary jazz.* Replacing the contemporary essays, Michael added a book about jazz's migration from Harlem and New Orleans to Kansas City in the 1930s.

A primate expert who loves jazz is a convincing character, Michael thought, *but it's not enough to make real money.* He would need to add another dimension: fly-fishing. A jazz-loving, fly-fishing geneticist? It wasn't a perfect fit, but he'd found the fly-fishing books the week before at a thrift store up in Albany. Michael arranged the books inside the box. He combed the thin strands of gray hair from the back of his head over the top. A fresh shirt might've helped, but Michael decided it would cut against whatever pity he might arouse in the buyer, so he left the house as he usually did, flecked with mustard.

❧

Michael's red pickup puttered along in the right-hand lane of the freeway between Eugene and Portland, reaching speeds as high as sixty miles per hour. As he drove, he would reach into the breast pocket of his suit coat and fish for a loose nut to crunch in his mouth, one at a time. Peanuts, mainly, with an occasional almond. When he got to Portland, Michael circled Powell's until a parking spot appeared and then plugged the meter with coins, terrified of getting pinched by the parking cops. *The fuzz,* he called them. In the bed of his truck, he'd open the box of books and arrange them again, choosing the titles that the buyer would see first and burying the more obscure primate books to be discovered like hidden gems. He made sure the jazz books stayed together to form a coherent story.

Michael winked at the fly-fishing books to give them luck, gathered up the box, and made his way into the store. He joined the line for the buyer's table and watched the buyer work. He was a younger man, with thick glasses and the grim purposefulness of someone who'd hoped to apply his literature degree in more meaningful ways. At Powell's, he was the gatekeeper of the store's collection. His judgment would decide what made it to the shelves, and whether Michael would have anything to show for his work.

Whether buyers care that they are buying from scouts, as opposed to readers or collectors, is a question that tugs at the paranoid imagination of every book scout. The job of the book buyer, especially at Powell's, which does a volume of business too large to be personal, is to choose books of high quality, nothing more. While a small bookstore might cultivate relationships with its customers by occasionally repurchasing books, there is no reason why a large bookstore would care if books came directly from readers or from scouts. On the other hand, buyers are human beings, and human beings like stories, and sometimes the story of the seller matters as much as the books they're selling.

When he was finally called forward, Michael, with the confidence of a fly-fishing primate scholar, casually presented his box of books for inspection. The buyer opened the box and removed the jazz books first, placing them all together in a neat pile at his side. Michael began to worry that this first pile was the one to be discarded. Then, one by one, the buyer started lifting the fly-fishing books out of the box, setting most of them into a pile next to the jazz books, and setting others, after scrutinizing their copyright pages and condition, in a pile at the edge of the table, near Michael. Those must be the discards, Michael inferred, his heart beating a little faster at the thought that the jazz books and most of the fly-fishing books would make the cut.

Finally, the buyer pulled the rest of the books from the box and looked quizzically at the highly technical tomes on primate reproduction and genetics, and then at Michael. Michael's blue eyes held steady as the buyer's question hung between them. The buyer let go, looked back down at the books, and began to scrutinize each one, down to its table of contents.

Michael's heart pounded, but he stood utterly still, following the buyer's eyes, watching carefully for signs. Finally, after inspecting each of the books, the buyer looked up.

"I don't know what to do with these," he said.

"They're about DNA," Michael said. "DNA and monkeys."

"Primates," the buyer said.

"Primates."

The buyer slowly pushed the entire pile of monkey books toward Michael, along with just a few of the fly-fishing books.

"I can't use these," he said.

"Okay." Michael never tried to negotiate.

With a pencil that had rested on his ear, the buyer made a tally on his notepad. "For the jazz books and the fishing books, I can do eighty."

"Okay," Michael said.

"Come back any time with jazz," the buyer said.

"Jazz," Michael said. "Okay."

The buyer reached under his desk and retrieved a logbook and asked Michael to inscribe his name and address, and to sign his name next to the payment amount. As Michael signed, the buyer rang his register and removed four $20 bills. They felt wonderful in Michael's hand, like a magic trick, converting old books into fresh new pieces of paper.

❧

Michael packed the discarded books back into the box and hurried back to his car. He would have to hustle to make this trip to Portland worth it. He drove across the bridge and east down Hawthorne Avenue, parking outside a satellite branch that Powell's had opened for its more eccentric eastside customers. The staff, including its buyers, reflected the area's quirkiness. While they were typically more selective than the downtown buyers, it wasn't obvious how the Hawthorne buyers decided which books to accept or reject.

Before Michael brought his discards into the store, he freshened the box up with handfuls of paperback fiction that he kept in his trunk, a mix of Steinbeck and Faulkner that he could always find at the thrift store, and that the bookstore would keep in stock. Once the box was ready, he brought it inside the store and presented it at the main counter, where nobody waited in line. The clerk called over to the buyer, another balding man who had wild tufts of white beard tumbling down from his face. The buyer eyed Michael sternly.

“Cash or credit?” the man barked.

“Cash or credit,” Michael repeated, unable to process the question before the words came out.

“Okay,” the man answered. “Come back in ten minutes.”

Without resolving the question of cash or credit, Michael walked away from the counter, leaving the man to unpack and sort through the books. This was the practice at smaller bookstores—customers could choose cash or a higher total in store credit to use on books they found while browsing. Michael needed money more than books, but to give the buyer time to consider his box, he retreated to the poetry section.

He began scanning the shelves alphabetically, looking for familiar names. In poetry, Michael’s blue eyes traveled along their familiar route, from Corso to di Prima, Ferlinghetti, and Ginsberg, stopping to check for Bob Kaufman before visiting McClure and Meltzer, hopping over to the two Kenneths, Patchen and Rexroth, always pausing for Snyder, and finally, to Welch and Whalen. There were other poets whose books were more valuable, but this was the path Michael took through every book store’s poetry section.

In between books of verse by James Dickey and John Donne, Michael plucked a volume from the shelf, thin enough that it didn’t have a title on the spine. On the cover page, he found three thick strokes of calligraphy, along with the publisher’s price for the book—ninety-five cents—and a familiar name: Diane di Prima. Michael knew that di Prima’s books were desirable. It was around that time that he was routinely subjected to my adolescent enthusiasm for her work.

The title of this crisp volume now in Michael’s hands itself could be read like a poem: *This Kind of Bird Flies Backward*. Michael knew, because he hadn’t seen it before, that this book was rare. It was her first book—and also the first to be published, in 1958—with the imprint of Totem Press. On its first page, the book had been signed by di Prima herself.

Michael set the book in its place on the shelf, deeper between the

Dickey and Donne than he'd found it, and returned to the buyer's counter to learn his fate. There, the stern man waited, having left most of the books in the box, with one tall stack in front of him.

"I can give you $30 cash or $35 in trade for the monkey books."

Michael weighed the offers. If he took the cash, he'd come home with more than $100, even if he stopped for a sandwich. If he took the trade credit, he'd have to spend another five dollars of his own cash to buy the di Prima and would come home with $75, without the sandwich. Once he accounted for gas it would be more like $50, and that didn't include the cost of the books themselves, or of Michael's time.

"Cash," Michael said, this time definitively. He accepted the $30 and left the store with his rejected books. On the way home, a thought tugged at Michael. It was di Prima's first book, published in a small run, one of the earliest such volumes exemplary of the Beat Generation. If he let the book get away, it could haunt Michael for months, maybe years. He would need to go back to Portland with a plan in place to secure the di Prima.

❧

By the time he'd arrived back home, Michael had worked out a plan. Rather than returning with a fresh batch of books and betraying his character, the primate scholar, he'd send in a proxy, say, a student bound for college who would incidentally trade a curated selection of books for a thin, obscure volume of Beat poetry. Michael would provide the books for me to trade, and I'd secure the di Prima. In this way also it would be a kind of rite of passage, to set me up with a book of significance and value as I ventured toward adulthood.

I was seventeen when Michael found *This Kind*. I'd started climbing my own mountains: finishing high school and taking early college classes, trying on other kinds of first love. I'd begun sorting through the books I'd accumulated in my childhood, keeping the set about cricket and my first edition of *Ball Four*, thinning some of the Beat poetry, and giving books I cared less about to Michael to sell. When he came home and told me about his find, I was excited, though maybe not like I would've been just a year or two earlier. Still, I agreed to make the trip back to Portland with him.

He helped me pack a box for Powell's, with some saleable nonfiction plus a few volumes of fiction and poetry, to paint a portrait of me as a precocious seventeen-year-old. I was to go to the counter at the Powell's on Hawthorne and explain that my uncle had given me his books about mushroom foraging, and that I wanted the trade credit to get books I'd need for college. Like most everything we did, it was an unnecessarily elaborate ruse in search of scant profit.

The buyer took my books without asking any questions. Necessary or not, our approach worked.

I plucked *This Kind* from where Michael had buried it on the shelf. Even as I'd grown more cynical as a teenager, I could feel its magic in my hands. The book had been printed in New York forty years earlier, in batches so small that di Prima and Amiri Baraka would've handled each volume. I knew she'd held this copy because it had her signature on the first page. The pen stroke was clean and simple, elegant, matching the delicate book.

Back home, I tucked *This Kind* safely into Michael's encased shelf, knowing that I'd be moving away from home. It would be there for me to come back to. Truth is, between my fear of creasing the spine and other concerns I had at seventeen, I didn't bother to read the poems inside. What mattered more to me was that our family would have something rare that we could hold onto.

CHAPTER 6

Michael's Books

Every honest scout's dream is to open a bookstore. It's encoded in their behavior: to accumulate a viable stock, scrape together just enough money for a space, hang on for a year or two, then retreat to scouting. Along the way, if you're lucky, you find something special, like a treasured copy of *This Kind of Bird Flies Backward.* Most of the time, you do what you have to do so that you can eat and pay the bills.

Michael's first bookstore was a blanket he set down on the patio outside the cafeteria at Fairhaven College back in Bellingham, Washington. It had no shelves or sections, only a selection of books Michael had found or borrowed. Since he started out with no money, he didn't expect to make any, either, which was a liberating way to operate his first business.

Michael's customers at the Fairhaven College setup included people whose relationships with the norms of officialdom mirrored his own. These were students who took classes for the purposes of qualifying for student loans, with or without intentions to eventually earn a degree. They found the most valuable lessons in experiences outside the classroom, achieving what education reformers would eventually call transformative learning. They lived and worked on farms or crashed with friends, and when they'd saved enough money, or if they had the right parents, they traveled.

In this context, selling books outside the cafeteria was a definite occupation, and Michael was a professional. He began to understand the kinds of books his customers would pick up, inspect, and occasionally buy, and then devised strategies to obtain those books. He would check thrift stores for thin folios of poetry. At garage sales he bargained for the kinds of nonfiction—books about growing mushrooms and wilderness living—that Fairhaven's students required.

He was also a reader and connoisseur of literary culture, in his way. He read deeply about the world wars, prime ministers, and blues and jazz music. He collected the posters for every reading and play offered at Fairhaven College for all the years he was in Bellingham. He kept copies of *The Wizard of Oz* and *Old Yeller*, books that had shaped his childhood, and across decades, whenever business was slow, Michael read from them.

On days when Michael sold a book, he had never been so sure that he'd found his occupation in life. The book represented value; it wasn't something you felt attached to. Though transactions often required social graces that weren't intuitive to Michael, he learned just enough to get by. The reward, while not remunerative, was a wad of crinkled bills far beyond what Michael had ever expected for himself. In this way, he was freshly satisfied with every sale. Even on days when he made no sales, which was most of them, he was happy to be outside, among college students, with the covers of interesting books looking up at him. There was no such thing as a bad day in the used book business.

Needing a fixed location for his store, Michael rented a train caboose, which doubled from time to time as his abode. In Fairhaven, before its boom years, an intrepid entrepreneur had arranged three retired train cars in a parking lot, creating the kind of business that would be the envy of Portland's economy of carts and pods decades later. Michael spotted the "for rent" sign in the window of the caboose, scraped a few dollars together, and opened for business. This was Michael's store when I met him. I loved it, and I can see now why my mom did also.

As a bookstore, the caboose was nearly perfect to showcase Michael's humble but growing collection. The daylight through the windows of the caboose created a cheerful ambience for shoppers, scant as they were. To enter the store, customers would climb up the stairs of the caboose like they were leaving town. Michael, the conductor, would hoist open the door.

Once inside, you had no choice but to engage with the books that Michael had set out. There was nowhere for customers to go except directly down the store's only aisle, until they reached the register at the end of the car. A savvy customer might start at the counter and work back to the door, facilitating an easy escape; most did not. Once a customer had entered the caboose, they had better buy a book or confront Michael, in all his awkwardness, with a worthy excuse.

Not that buying a book from Michael was difficult or unpleasant. The books were modestly priced, with few exceeding the total cost of a coffee and a cinnamon roll from Tony's, the café down the street. A customer might reason that she or he would rather have the spiritual nourishment of an ex-library edition of Alan Watts than the fleeting material comfort of the caffeine and empty carbs from the café. A fortunate customer might afford both: a dog-eared book from the caboose in the warm embrace of a comfy chair at Tony's.

That customers didn't stream into the caboose in great numbers didn't trouble Michael, nor was he bothered by his modest totals at the end of the day. Having few financial commitments besides the rent of the caboose, which was priced appropriately, he needed only a handful of sales each week to make his margin. Because he didn't pay for housing, the margin was needed only to satisfy Michael's belly.

As a dwelling, the caboose lacked several important features. It had no kitchen, which was mitigated by Tony's cinnamon rolls. Sell a book and you could afford a raisin-stuffed roll. Sell two and you could have coffee with it, with lots of cream. The problem was that the caboose lacked a restroom or any other kind of running water, meaning that Michael occasionally had to close the shop out of necessity.

Despite its inconveniences, the success Michael experienced at the caboose stamped him forever as a businessman. Among the lessons he learned: A bookstore can be anything, and anything can be a bookstore, and a good day of work is when you make enough to eat. Occasionally, something extraordinary would happen. Michael was operating the store in the caboose when he met Diane at the professor's party. Soon after they met, he showed us around the store—the first bookstore I remember. For a five-year-old, a bookstore inside a train caboose was magical, and Michael, in my eyes, was a special person.

Michael opened his next store in downtown Bellingham, this time in a proper building with running water and a bathroom. To save money, Michael made a home for me and my mom in the bookstore, with a shabby couch down at the bottom of the dark storeroom, and up above it, a lofted space with a bed, illuminated by a lamp that drew power from an extension cord that ran all the way to the front of the bookstore. For dinner we had piles of teriyaki chicken with extra portions of rice from the takeout place on the corner. Every hour I was not in school was spent inside a bookstore, the only catch being that I was not to mention it to my teacher or anyone else at the elementary school.

Tired of this life, my mom did what so many others have done, from the Steinbeck characters who fled the Dust Bowl to the exasperated Californians looking for a life they could afford: we moved to Oregon. My mom found work in Salem, and we filled our car and rented the first house we saw. Michael followed after he closed his shop and sorted his affairs. He brought only his most valuable books, leaving the rest behind in store-closing sales and then offloading the remains to other dealers.

In Oregon, Michael became a scout in its purest form, buying from thrift stores and library sales and selling to Powell's, most often with me in tow. It was not an elegant operation, not the life you might imagine when you think of rare books—the erudite, antiquarian dealer with a pipe and patches on his jackets. We traveled in cars with mechanical problems to thrift stores run by humans often in no better condition. When we did well, we would stop at a Chinese restaurant inside an office building that charged only $1 for a scoop of any dish. I only wanted beef with broccoli, two scoops. The mustard was too spicy for Michael.

Michael found part-time work in Portland with David Morrison, who sold books out of a warehouse space on the east side of town, decades before it became cool. David specialized in art and photography, though he badgered his customers with beliefs and opinions that would sound insane anywhere outside of Southeast Portland. Coming home from his shifts, Michael told us stories about David ranting at customers, mostly about conspiracies that David had read about in books he collected. He was decades ahead of his time. Eventually, David fired Michael for describing a book about personality based on sibling birth order as "woo woo."

Michael cobbled together enough books to open another bookstore, this time in downtown Salem, where there were few readers, but also where, at the time, there were no other bookstores. In those days, Michael seemed, at least to me, like a person of importance in our city. His store was visited by Salem's literati, mostly men (like me, eventually) who hid their eccentricities from the state agencies that employed them, finding comfort and kinship between covers. Then there were the washed-up musicians and artists who couldn't keep up with the Portland scene, preferring instead the dive bars and social services of the mid-valley. One such example was John Fahey, a legendary guitarist who came to occupy the unused office space above Michael's store, working on a novel that would never be published. As a teenager, I spent my after-school hours around Fahey, who, like me at that time, had nowhere better to go.

The store in downtown Salem was called Michael's Books, representing the chapter in Michael's life when he took pride in his craft, and the eponym suited him. The business had been launched with my mom's credit cards, which paid for the wood and nails we used to build shelves. Even the deftest accountant would never be able to discern whether the operation ever became profitable. Michael actually had an accountant, and he was deft, but the better part of the accountant's counsel was spent on strategies to avoid taxation on Michael's earnings. Years later, I caught a glimpse of the letter sent to Michael by the Social Security Administration, documenting his annual earnings across the decades of his career. The high point, reaching five figures but only barely, came during the early nineties at Michael's Books.

And then it was time for us to move again, to a small farmhouse on the outskirts of Monmouth, a farm town too small to have outskirts, really. Monmouth was between Salem, where Diane worked, and Corvallis, where Michael opened his next bookstore. He leased a large space in downtown Corvallis in partnership with an old acquaintance from Bellingham, Walt Oldham. Walt had been involved in Michael's early bookstores and, having run unsuccessfully for city council a handful of times in Bellingham, decided to hitch his fortunes to ours. In Corvallis, it was Walt who lived in the bookstore. The store had a basement where Walt kept his bed and, beside it, a loaded revolver. As a teenager exploring Michael's store, I came across the gun before retreating upstairs.

It was in Corvallis that we got to know Gerry Rouff. Gerry had been in Oregon for over a decade by the time we arrived, picking up shifts at the town's big store, the Book Bin, and publishing his own catalog of books that interested few buyers, mainly selling literature in translation. Gerry claimed he'd never be crazy enough to open his own store. Instead, he became a steady presence in Michael's store, though it was unclear, even to Michael, whether he was working or hanging around. If he got paid, it was in books. Any cash the store made was siphoned out by Walt, who had developed the habit of visiting Squirrel's Tavern most nights, and always on nights when belly dancers graced the bar. This way of life was sustained for only a year before the operation became too unmanageable to go on, and the Corvallis store closed, leaving Michael, once again, to make his living by scouting the thrift stores and selling to Powell's.

Michael opened his final store in Eugene, where he and Diane settled together around the time I set out on my own. In Eugene, Michael opened Balcony Books in a building shared by a hairdresser and a group of Alcoholics Anonymous, across the street from the bus mall. Michael spent his days curating his last and best selection of books for a clientele that was mostly unhoused or trying to stay warm between bus transfers.

Diane was diagnosed with breast cancer, requiring Michael to focus on her treatment and care, and through sheer luck, he received an unsolicited offer to sell his store to a stranger who had always wanted to run a bookstore but didn't know much about the business. Michael came to an agreement with the buyer on a price, modest but enough to support himself and Diane through the course of her treatment. After several months, Michael noticed that the bookstore no longer opened for business, and he found, at regular intervals, boxes of books from the store left on the porch of his house by his successor. Michael remained in the book business without a storefront, selling his old books online and shipping them off to customers around the world from the post office next to the train station in downtown Eugene.

❧

The nature of Michael's business was that something good would drift in and then, when necessity demanded, Michael would let it go. This was true of nearly everything in Michael's life—his bookstores and the books themselves, his houses and apartments, his clothes, his pets, his cars, and most of his wives. How did my mom and I stick around for so long, I wonder, when everything around us was left behind in service of the search for the next thing?

That di Prima volume, *This Kind of Bird Flies Backward*, became part of our family's story. It was the great find of Michael's career, around which so much of our lives had been arranged. I was sure that it would stay with us, that one day it would be the jewel in my own collection. Bookstores had come and gone, but this book had the potential to stick.

The further I wandered out into the world, the idea that I would possess *This Kind* served to anchor me to the family I came from. I could move on from the chaotic life, the constant moves and openings and closings of stores, the towers of books in our living spaces, and the jarring rhythms of sales and fairs. But *This Kind* was solid, worth holding onto.

And then we sold it. Michael had listed the book online at a price so high that if someone tried to buy it, it would be a good problem to have. I was at college, a few years away from home, when $500 may as well have been the moon. To the buyer on the other end of the digital transaction, it was a fair price for an exceptional book. When the order came in, Michael called me on the landline at my college in Vermont to discuss it.

"I never thought anyone would buy it," he said.

"Is it even worth that much?" I asked.

"Depends," he said. "I guess if you have money, it's worth it."

"I mean, what really matters is the poetry, right? The book itself is just paper," I said.

"There are a lot of books out there," Michael said. We manufactured, through dubious reasoning, the sense that we could replace the book if we ever needed to.

We talked about the price and how we'd divide the proceeds. A portion of the sale would go into my bank account to use for food and rent at a time when I needed the help. The book was shipped off to a stranger and gone from our lives.

CHAPTER 7

Nonfiction

Rounding the bend into my forties, with wiry hairs sticking out of my own increasingly bulbous forehead, I've accumulated enough jobs and titles that my apprenticeship with Michael is buried deep beneath the newer editions of my life's story. I am a partner to a person who, though she loves to read, is indifferent to where her books come from. She would order the latest Zadie Smith from ThriftBooks and then look at me with amused tolerance when I brought home a first edition of *White Teeth*, like a pet showing off its catch. I am a father of two boys who now read for themselves. I also get public employee benefits, meaning my future is secure enough that I have no need to drag my own kids to library sales. If Michael's lessons stuck, they're down at the bottom of my life's box of books, beneath the tomes of my family and career.

For years I didn't think about *This Kind*, or, if the thought came creeping in, I reminded myself that owning something, even something so precious, mattered little relative to the value of my education, which the sale had helped to support. In that sense, it might be possible to let go of the regret I felt. But as my career began in earnest and the price of that sale became dwarfed by my monthly income, the question of what it might mean to own a copy of the book came back to me—the gut punch of middle age. You scrap, you get a job, you want something to show for it before time wins again. In my case, it wasn't a car or a watch, but the ache to possess something essential to my understanding of the family I came from.

I began searching for *This Kind* online but found it painful even to type the title into a search engine. When I did gather the nerve, what I learned didn't help. The original edition, the one that Michael and I had owned, was printed and assembled by di Prima herself, by hand. There might be a few dozen of these books left on the planet, and these would remain on the shelves of collectors until they died. A university library had started leveraging its resources to buy up di Prima's works and papers. More would follow. Eventually, if it wasn't already, the book would become truly unobtainable.

I knew it would be impossible to obtain *This Kind* in the way that Michael had. I wanted no part of arranging a box of books, schlepping it up to a store in Portland, waiting in line, presenting myself for a buyer's scrutiny, and then, with any luck, walking away with a fistful of dollars and a still mostly full box. Powell's doesn't pay cash anymore, but even if I could still get $40 for a box of books, what would I do with it? Pay exactly 0.007 percent of my mortgage? Even on a public employee's salary, it doesn't move the needle. I wondered how scouts like Michael still existed. Even though there are plenty of readers in the world, the number of books a scout would need to sell to support himself today is beyond practical reach.

I have the privilege of seeing both worlds—the book scout's precarity, and the more traditional, middle-class path that comes with a retirement plan. When I choose to revisit Michael's world, I know that it's a vacation, time-bound, and with no obligation to stay. I also know—from my day job as a policy analyst for the state legislature—some of the damning statistics that illustrate what Michael and other book scouts are up against. In a sense, I feel like a spy among book scouts, knowing the secrets of their world, but with my own life to return home to.

In a statistic relevant to my work, I learned that the average monthly rent paid by older Oregonians, including the last generation of scouts, is $1,075. For those lucky enough to own their homes, the remaining mortgage payments, taxes, and home insurance are more than twice the cost of renting. The major expense, along with food, clothing, and other necessities, is health care, including, for most folks, Medicare premiums. For any aging book scout who still makes the rounds to thrift stores and sales, you would also need income sufficient for a car, including insurance and gas.

On the other side of the ledger, assume, generously, that the median-priced book resold at Powell's is $15, and that Powell's would pay a scout $5 for it. Just to pay the cost of rent in Oregon, without accounting for health care, food, or transportation, a scout would have to sell Powell's no fewer than 215 books each month. I knew that Michael wasn't doing this kind of volume. If book scouts still existed, I'm not sure how they could make any kind of living.

I found a book—and ordered it online—to help me answer the question. In *The Last Bookseller*, Gary Goodman argues that both scouts and bookstores are on the brink of extinction. He draws on the early success and eventual failure of his store in Minnesota, St. Croix Antiquarian Books, to make his case that the internet changed the business. There's no doubting his statistics about the decline of brick-and-mortar stores. It's also true that digital commerce has changed every retail business, from shoes to pet shops, even if the survivors of these other sectors haven't written books on the subject.

On the edges of Goodman's story, I recognized patterns familiar to me from Michael and the scouts we'd known in Oregon. You scout books, open a store, and fail. And then you keep on scouting. Digital commerce didn't extinguish the business, convenient as that myth may be. The online marketplace forced brick and mortar stores to close, but it also removed barriers to doing business. People who would never qualify for a lease gained direct access to customers. Stores lost the autonomy to set prices. Instead, the market rewards true scarcity. The business has moved online but it hasn't gone away. Scouts who recognize what's truly rare will always have work.

Still, I worry about aging booksellers, even the ones who adapt. People like Michael and Diane, despite working their whole lives, will struggle to get the care they need to stay in their homes. It's true that Michael chose a career that was never lucrative, that never promised stability. Though I'm not sure he'd have kept a more formal job, he got to do work he loved every day. My mom also did work she cared about, but she worked herself to the bone to keep her job and retired to avoid being laid off. Now, they will choose between food and prescriptions. As their care needs increase, the safety net to catch them, the state's program for aging people with disabilities, is weak and full of holes.

It will, we know, get worse. In policy literature it's been described as the "silver tsunami"—the question of how society will care for a cresting wave of people now reaching retirement age without a system of support or a workforce to provide the care. It falls on family members who may or may not have the skills or resources, including time, to help loved ones age with dignity. This will come for us all.

The money that Michael makes from books barely dents the cost of living, much less health care. Michael declined to pursue his doctor's referral for physical therapy for his shuffling when he learned he'd have to pay $35, more than he might expect to get from selling a box of books to Smith Family. Policies are unforgiving to people who work nontraditional jobs, especially if, like bookselling, the work isn't particularly lucrative. It can be more precarious than having nothing, which at least allows people to qualify for certain kinds of assistance. That Michael and Diane have their own house, humble as it is, is a complicated blessing. Without the money to make repairs, it grows older and less livable. If they ever do need a higher level of care, they will have to spend down what remains of their money before qualifying, and then, when they pass, the state can come for their home.

Though I don't need to keep the house after they're gone, I have this desire to preserve it somehow, with the wall-to-wall bookshelves and maybe even some of the chaos intact. I imagine keeping the house in its current state, but without people in it. It would be quiet except for the rotary phone my parents have always kept. When I need to know what a book is worth, maybe somehow it will let me call Michael.

CHAPTER 8

Myths & Texts

If the fate of my parents didn't keep me up at night, my rumination turned to *This Kind of Bird Flies Backward.* I would lie awake picturing the book that got away, plotting to get it back. I could scarcely remember the copy we had sold, and so, for me, it became something more than paper or even poetry. I imagined holding it, to shield it from the perpetual decline of the material, middle-aged world around me—the last perfect thing.

I conjured the cover of *This Kind* as something like its more common siblings, like the first Totem Press printing of Gary Snyder's *Myths & Texts.* For Snyder's book, Baraka had risked a larger print run, and you could still find it in stores for $50. It's a thin, humble little book, with thick brush strokes that form the M and T in the book's title, paired incongruently with a blocky font. *This Kind* would be wrapped in the same soft, white cover, but without the clumsy strokes on Snyder's book. The title would be set in a confident font to say, *Here I am, a poet with something to declare.* There would be an illustration—a solid, abstract shape, almost but not quite perfectly formed. The artist's hand would slip just enough to betray di Prima's uncertainty, the crushing weight of beauty yet to see itself.

Inside, the publisher's page would include only some opaque clues about the existence of Totem Press, maybe the address of someone's apartment in New York. Totem Press was more a concept than a publishing house. Its headquarters were the Greenwich Village cafés where Baraka could be found cavorting with poets. Its office was the pages of the *Floating Bear*, the early newsletter published by di Prima and Baraka, where they asked, *What is art? Who decides?*

This Kind of Bird Flies Backward was their first attempt at an answer. But di Prima would not have waited for Baraka or anyone else to tell her that her book was good enough to publish. She knew that she was a poet, and that the next and only right thing for her to do was to publish her work. It didn't matter where or how, only that the poetry would find its way out into the world. She didn't need permission.

I imagined her poems would feel like this, like first love. They would echo di Prima's desperate love for Baraka in the fall of 1958, when he was married and just out of reach to her. This is the thing you want to possess—not the $500 book, but the feeling of finding it for $35. Not the poetry inside, but the unopened mystery on the shelf. The lifelong quest for one book makes the most sense when you've never read it—when its contents are whatever you've dreamt them to be.

❧

Michael never felt at ease in another person's bookstore unless he was reselling, so I was surprised when he suggested that we check out Browsers' Bookstore in Albany, an hour north of home in Eugene. After a couple of decades away from Oregon, and from Michael's universe, I'd recently moved back to Eugene, with my family, following the COVID-19 pandemic. We'd rented an apartment downtown, close enough to the Whiteaker to see Michael and my mom as often as we needed to. We figured we would buy a house and settle into a neighborhood once we determined the right proximity to them. On the weekends, Michael and I were relearning how to be around each other. Having raised me to fluency in the tongue of used books, Michael called to me in our lost language, and I answered.

I found Michael's network of people and bookstores mostly intact. Over the last twenty years, Michael had been up to Browsers' Bookstore a handful of times, dropping in to chat with Gerry Rouff. After Browsers' opened, Gerry became the right hand of its owner, Scott Givens. Gerry started by working on catalogs, then as a book buyer for Browsers', identifying books with value and listing them online. He was gradually retiring when Scott decided, after twenty years, to sell the Albany store to Abe Richmond, a younger Browsers' employee. Even after he quit working, Gerry still hung around the store, brought books of interest to sell to Abe, and shared a kind word about Browsers' when he made his regular phone calls to scouts around the Willamette Valley. Gerry was the social tissue connecting bookstore owners to each other's lives.

From Gerry, Michael heard that the new Browsers' Bookstore, reopened under Abe, was worth visiting. According to Gerry, Abe had inherited the store from Scott, who was like a father and mentor to Abe. Also, according to Gerry, Abe was crazy because you would have to be if you wanted to run a used bookstore. Gerry had never opened his own store. Instead, he sharpened his sense of nuance by reading avant-garde fiction in translation until it was no longer avant-garde, seasoning his perspective. Abe was too naïve to make it as a bookseller, Gerry said. He was also the profession's only hope for the future.

When Michael suggested that we make the trip up to Albany to see Browsers' for ourselves, I imagined it would be like every other trip we had taken in search of books: Michael would scour the shelves for books that he could sell online for a modest profit. The problem with this approach, in the digitized age, is that the books in Browsers' and almost every other store are already listed online. Despite the skepticism I'd acquired in middle age, I still hoped that searching for books with Michael, on a tip from Gerry, could yield something unexpected. I nurtured the fantasy that Michael would again lead me to another overlooked volume of di Prima to replace the one we'd sold.

Michael asked me to drive. He didn't care much for driving anymore, not on highways, or in fog, or to destinations beyond the grocery store and the pharmacy. Michael's world had shrunk in his seventh decade. So, when he called me on a Saturday morning, having decades ago seeded in me the itch to look for books, I was glad to swing by his old house and pick him up in my Prius. Just as Michael's rattling red pickup announced his arrival at thrift stores up and down the valley, the Prius makes its presence known on the streets with its bureaucratic efficiency, using gas but not too much gas, moving fast but not too fast. It would make the perfect getaway car, not because it would outrun anyone, but because nobody would suspect its involvement in a heist—or a well-executed scouting of Browsers' Bookstore.

As we drove, Interstate 5 yawned between Eugene and Albany, slowing down for men like Michael and me on our Saturday expedition. Cruising at ten miles below the speed limit, I watched the sheep out my window, standing in their field, watching me back. The sun broke through the clouds, beaming through the windshield. When I looked over at Michael, I could see in full relief the progress of his wrinkles as they advanced across his face, having won their various battles across his forehead and the corners of his eyes. Michael's window framed the foothills of the Cascades, with snowy peaks creating a textured background for my view of Michael's prominent nose.

We arrived at Browsers' just as it was set to open. The store itself resembled a one-story residential home built in the 1950s—a rambler, you'd call it—but in a neighborhood that was paved over when Albany attempted to impose a perverse kind of order on its traffic patterns, weaving the industrial and agricultural traffic of the old Highway 99E through an historic neighborhood, creating incongruous city blocks of strip malls and single-family homes.

While the bookstore had settled into the rambler, the rambler had never been remodeled or adapted from its original use to accommodate a bookstore. You walk into the store through the house's living room, but where you might expect a sofa, you find a desk stacked high with books, and on either side of the desk, shelves up to the ceiling. It's like being in your grandparents' house, except that it also happens to be a used bookstore.

From the living room you have options: you may remain among the stacks of fiction, turn right into the dining room that science fiction shares with biography, or wander to the left, along a wall of paperback mystery and into the kitchen, where military history and westerns mingle by the sink. Continue further to the back bedroom and you find romance, messy stacks of pink covers strewn about like an unmade bed.

To be inside another bookseller's store, for me, was like meeting someone I could have been. I could track every marginal decision, every book picked up at a sale or bought back from a customer. From a book's price, marked in pencil in the top right corner of the fly leaf, I could infer a sense of the seller's own self-worth. The layout of a store reveals elements of character: if fiction is at the center of the store despite its unprofitability, the bookseller is a reader, maybe too much of one to endure. If the cold, hard facts of hardback nonfiction take center stage, then the bookseller is a businessperson, maybe too joyless to stick around when sales are slow. It's impossible for me to walk through a store without studying each of these choices, thinking about what I'd have done. I wondered, as I did this, what kind of bookseller I might be. What habits would I have learned from Michael and the stores where I lurked?

Michael, needing to find his bearings at Browsers', to orient himself to the logic of the store, started with the biography section. He always felt at ease among the familiar personages of the twentieth century. Biography seldom produces a valuable find, with one exception: you never know when an autograph has been overlooked by a bookseller, and for certain celebrities, the value can be hundreds of dollars. I recalled, as Michael had trained me, that large bookstores like Powell's are famous for this. For the scout, the only downside is that, to find the overlooked signature you must search the first pages of every single book of interest. Michael began this project in earnest.

I left Michael and went to look for the poetry books in the living room, where I found an ornate volume by Rainer Maria Rilke, a poem about the Virgin Mary that had been published by the University of California Press in 1947, after he'd become known for less overtly religious work. The book's gold dust jacket matched the speckled ceiling of the store. It looked like it could be valuable—a first printing of Rilke, in hardcover—but on closer inspection, the dust jacket was tarnished. I could hear Michael's voice in my head as he looked at books across the room: condition is everything. As canonical as Rilke may be, some posthumously published verses about the Virgin Mary, not good enough to circulate in the poet's lifetime, would interest only the most desperate completist. Fool's gold. Instead, I reached for a paperback collection of poetry by Tomas Tranströmer, published in the 1970s with introductions by Robert Bly. Even though it was a trade edition with flimsy wrappers, it was out of print, and readers—me included—would want it for the poetry.

The Rilke would likely remain at Browsers' for another decade, until a genuine Rilke collector, a person rarer than the book itself, happened upon it. The Tranströmer, on the other hand, with its clever, straightforward verses, would have a market. It would take only one of the students from the creative writing program at the university to stop by and nourish his or her soul with Tranströmer for the price of a cup of coffee. I had forgotten nothing that Michael had taught me: I could still see how scarcity informed the value in a book, and it still thrilled me.

Michael had wandered from the living room to the kitchen, where he looked for volumes of World War II history to resell, or so I had assumed. When I found him, he was reading from a collection of letters written by Winston Churchill, so engaged with the book that I wondered if it wasn't for resale. What would a book scout want with the old Bulldog's letters? Maybe it was the cold comfort of the expired twentieth century, the good fight. Squint hard enough and you might see a bit of Churchill in Michael—a singular and unyielding orientation to the world. Or, at least when he was younger, the round belly.

I left Michael on the battlefield and retreated to the living room. At the center of the room, where the fireplace had been carved out to create a nook lined with bookshelves, I found Abe Richmond, the young man who had bought the bookstore, sitting at his desk. He matched the image I'd sketched in my mind's eye based on Michael's summary of Gerry's description. Abe's face was young, maybe the youngest bookseller I'd ever seen, but his youth was obscured by the armor of his thick glasses. He looked more Portland than Albany, which is to say, his black T-shirt paid homage to an obscure foreign movie director instead of the Second Amendment. The glasses and T-shirt, and the fact that he was wearing his raincoat inside in the bookstore, in the middle of the day, gave Abe the rugged, ill-at-ease handsomeness that settles on young men grown up in the Pacific Northwest.

Abe stood at the counter at the center of the store, alert in case he was needed by a customer. Though he'd worked at the store since before he was an adult, he was newly its proprietor, and perhaps the gravity of the business challenge had set in. Or maybe he was lost in thought. What would it be like to sit at the center of the rambler in Albany every day except Sundays and Mondays, nurturing your life's ambitions?

I paused in the doorway between the kitchen and the living room, with Michael and his Churchill behind me and Abe in front, staring ahead in thought. In my own life, I don't have the luxury of that gaze, the time to reach backward and work things out, or even to fret idly about the future. For me, it's work and kids and, on a good day, some sleep. I wondered about Abe's life, where he lived and what might lurk, at his young age, on his list of regrets. He was too young to have them, maybe, but he would never have to wonder what it would be like to run his own bookstore. In my stomach,

I sensed the same tug as when I thought about the di Prima that Michael had sold—the ache of something that got away.

When I approached Abe at his desk with Tranströmer in hand, he greeted me with the soft "Hello" of someone who is open to talking but who does not require a conversation; friendly but not burdensome.

"I wondered when somebody would find this," he said.

"I don't know much about Tranströmer," I said. I felt embarrassed, certain I was mispronouncing the poet's name, unsure what to say to the young bookseller.

"He won the Nobel, right? It's seven dollars."

"I think so," I said.

I paid Abe with cash. Even though used bookstores all take cards, I knew from Michael that cash remains king in transactions for used goods, perhaps for its transmutability, tax-wise. As Abe counted out the change, I absorbed as much as I could about the titles on the shelves in the carved-out fireplace nook behind him. It was hard to tell at first glance what he was collecting back there, but I noticed a shelf of thin volumes, maybe poetry.

"How's business since you took over?"

I regretted my question immediately. It's never polite to ask a bookseller about business. Still, Abe responded with grace.

"It's great," he said. "I get to hang out in a bookstore. It's a good business."

There was something here that I wanted more than the Tranströmer. Something about Abe, or his shop. The book scouts I'd known had no equanimity. But Abe didn't seem troubled. He wasn't threatened by customers or questions about his own business. I didn't doubt the sincerity of his answer.

"Got anything interesting back there?" I nodded to the shelves behind Abe.

Abe stepped to the side, allowing me to peer at the shelves behind him. He didn't hesitate to reveal his collection.

"I've been setting aside some postmodern fiction, some of the stuff that's getting reprinted now by the small presses." He pointed to a shelf with novels by John Barth, an author whose name sounded vaguely familiar but who has never been among my interests. "And then I do my own collecting with stuff I order online." He turned to another shelf, directing my eyes to a collection of works by Gary Snyder.

My stomach tightened. What was happening?

"You want to come back and look?" he asked.

I squeezed around the counter and stood next to Abe, the first time I'd been behind the counter of a bookseller who wasn't Michael. There, I stood face-to-face with a shelf of rare collections of Gary Snyder's poetry. Abe had first editions of some of Snyder's best books—*Turtle Island* and *Myths & Texts*. He had signed and numbered small press runs and broadsides. I love Snyder for his work but have never desired to collect him or to own the work completely in the way Abe's collection suggested. Then, next to Snyder, I saw something that made my heart jump: an early volume of *Revolutionary Letters*, a copy of the *Calculus of Variation*, and between them, a dozen or more books by Diane di Prima. Gently, breathlessly, I checked each thin volume. *Loba*, and *Memoirs of a Beatnik*. Then I saw it, with the deft calligraphy on the cover just as I'd imagined it: *This Kind of Bird Flies Backward*. I withdrew it from the shelf, held it, and quickly set it back on the shelf with the rest of Abe's collection without opening its cover.

"I—we had that once."

"Really? You like di Prima?"

"She's great," I said, retreating from behind the counter.

Michael was lurking now in the living room of the store, pawing at some fiction. I waved him to the counter and paid for his Churchill. I didn't want Michael to know about the copy of *This Kind*, to unearth that history we shared. Nor was I ready to talk to Abe, a stranger, about our relationship with the book. I wanted to escape the broken-down rambler so I could think and make sense of it all.

Abe watched us from the counter as we left abruptly with the book about Winston Churchill. "Come by whenever," he said.

CHAPTER 9

What Kyger Knew

Seeing Abe's collection of di Prima knocked something loose in me. Instead of the Zen calm I'd usually felt in my Prius, I started driving impatiently, speeding inadvertently as my thoughts raced. I'd been listening on repeat in my car's CD player to a band called Mount Eerie. If you grew up in the Pacific Northwest around the time I did, you know this band and its frontman, Phil Elverum, who also made music as The Microphones. Elverum will drive me nuts with a ten-minute song he wrote about his meditation retreat. Then when he layers his earnest observations into guitar feedback that sounds like the wind, it hits like a poem. As with my parents, I just can't let go.

One of my favorite songs quotes the poet Joanne Kyger. In the relevant lyric, Mount Eerie sings, "Joanne Kyger says, 'We fight incredibly through a hideous mishmash of inheritance / forgiving for deeper stamina. That we go on, the world / always goes on, breaking us with its changes / until our form, exhausted, runs true.'"

I could never make full meaning of this, except that it spoke to inheritance and change, two themes that resonate for me. The trip to Browsers' had awoken in me a network of connections, and I recalled the previous link between Kyger's world and my own search. She'd been married to Gary Snyder back in 1960—she was his first love, after mountains—and traveled with him to India and Japan. After they split and he found fame, she went on to write uncompromising poetry that transcended any association with Snyder. Her work endures, including in the music of Mount Eerie.

If you look for Kyger's books, you will rarely find anything other than the collection published by Penguin in the early 2000s. Even that volume, when you find it, is overpriced at $20 for a trade paperback. Kyger didn't publish prolifically. Unlike di Prima, she didn't reproduce her own books as a side hustle. Instead, in addition to a handful of small press runs and broadsides, she published four substantial volumes of collected poetry, about one for each decade she wrote.

Determined to read Kyger after hearing her poetry in a song, I ran headlong into the trap of the collector. I could buy the Penguin collection for $20, but it would give me only about a quarter of her poetry, a selection narrowed by some editor's whim. At the other extreme, Kyger's complete work had been collected in a hardback published by the National Poetry Foundation in 2007. The best version of this I could find from a reputable seller online was listed by Rural Hours, a dealer in Eastern Oregon, for $475.

To read Kyger, I would have to let the tiger out of the cage. I'd have to behave like a collector. I started by buying three of her four major collections that I'd found from a seller in Utah, Weller books. It was $70 for the three books, not cheap, but an investment in myself and my journey with Kyger. After I'd made my order, I kept searching, as one does, and realized that the same seller had the missing collection for $35.

My heart pounded. I began to worry that someone else would buy the fourth and missing piece in the minutes before I could contact Weller Books to amend my order. I imagined the internet as a frenzied place where people with unstable minds would gnash at poems written between 1980 and 1989 by a deceased, not-quite-Beat poet. The next morning, the minute that Weller Books was open, I called and explained the situation breathlessly.

The clerk had just arrived and sounded in need of coffee. She would have to consult with her colleagues about how to amend the order and would call me back. The minutes passed like hours as I waited. Finally, she called me back and explained that she'd be glad to take my credit card number and add the book to the order. They weren't in my hands yet, but I'd secured an understanding with Weller Books to send me the four significant collections of Joanne Kyger's body of work.

With the matter resolved, I took another look online at Kyger's books, as one does. Most were anthologies with one of her poems, or a broadside—basically a poster with a poem printed on it. There were a couple of journals she'd written while living abroad. At the end of the search results, on page nine, I found something of interest. It was, as confirmed by Wikipedia, Kyger's first book, *The Tapestry and the Web*. Published in 1965, it was a thin paperback published by the Four Seasons Foundation, which had brought the poets of the San Francisco renaissance out into the world. I'd seen Four Seasons books before, delicately printed in runs of about a thousand each. This just happened to be Kyger's first book, and according to the listing, it included a line of Kyger's poetry clipped from an original manuscript and pasted into the book: "Marigolds / who bit them off at the stems."

At this point, I was already $110 into Kyger, but an author's first work, manuscript inlaid, is the kind of book that defines a collection. If I were rational, I could've stopped my search at the Penguin collection, perfect for a reader and only $20. Instead, I chose to pursue Kyger deep into the wilds of the internet, a hunt that stretched from yesterday into this morning, involving multiple phone calls to Weller Books. So, my options were to stop now, with four volumes of Kyger spanning her career as a poet, or to double down and order her first book.

It wasn't a choice at all. I clicked through the order for Kyger's first book before someone else could beat me to it and paid for expedited shipping to ensure that it would be safely with me as soon as possible.

Though I now had four collections of Kyger along with her first book, I still had one problem. None of them was suitable to travel with, or to read casually in bed or the bath. To avoid the potential for water damage or coffee stains, I ordered the Penguin collection as my reading copy. This was the $20 solution I'd needed all along, found after spending $210, plus shipping, and two days of my spare time. The tiger's appetite had prevailed.

At this point in my life, I'm compelled to think about the path I didn't take, to feel it in tension with the life I've got. Not that I'm ungrateful for the pleasures that come free and easy—the satisfaction of a good night's rest, the gentle nudge of the morning's coffee. I like my life. But things get interesting when people come into contact with other people, when their dreams and ideas collide, where pathways diverge. For me, the friction is what matters, not the resolution.

My search for Kyger was deliciously fraught. Once I'd allowed that the Penguin collection wouldn't be enough, there was no stopping point to the desire that followed. I'd need every collection she published, and then her first book, and after all of that, I'd have to have the Penguin anyway. Even now, I'm thinking about ordering the National Poetry Foundation collection from Rural Hours. And then what? The broadsides, and then every anthology where one of her poems appears.

❧

Kyger would be mortified at the materialism her work provoked in me. When her books finally came in the mail, I tore through layers of thoughtful packaging, desperate to hold them. Inside, I found humble paperbacks designed to be read. Kyger's books were expensive not because they were particularly elegant but because they were rare. I should've known, and still, I felt disappointment.

With my enthusiasm muted, I began to read. I'd expected, like di Prima, that Kyger's verses would paint the Beat milieu—the classic cocktail of poverty and art with a dash of revolution. These were the goods I'd paid for, the hits that I'd come to the show to sing along to. I would ingest hundreds of dollars' worth of this serotonin that had been thoughtfully described and neatly packaged, and then I would place it on my shelf and forget about it.

What I found was something else: Kyger's poetry was the story of detachment over possession. From the first poem in her first published book, she gives us: "nothing promised that isn't shown." Kyger wasn't interested in the project of feeding my middle-aged desires. She wasn't serving tasty ambiguity or mapping untaken pathways. Instead, Kyger writes directly, clearly about letting go.

She lets go of possession itself ("I wrestled with the dragon / who holds the diamond jewel / of liberation. It came out / to wander in the big dome of living tissue"). Starting with her earliest poems, some written as she travelled with Gary Snyder to India and Japan, she lets go of ways of thinking ("cut through / and I can see all of this / and part of an idea too"). She lets go of the safety of ideas about home ("In this world that has got closed over by houses and networks, I fly out"). She lets go of her father ("it's impossible to know but blood does bring curiosity").

I thought of Michael, whose blood wasn't in me, but who had provoked more curiosity than anyone else ever had. Michael was all matter—all forehead and paunch, pastrami and mustard, books and more books. He doesn't wander in Kyger's dome of living tissue; he *is* the dome, the holder of things. But like Kyger, he had his own kind of wisdom. He didn't care about anything too much or grasp at a prescribed way of living. His ideas about home—a caboose, a bookstore, a small house—were those of someone who didn't need anything in particular. When the time came, he would let books go too.

I'd found everything I needed in Kyger's first book. The Penguin edition would've been enough too. I probably could've gotten it from the library. Instead of letting competing impulses of fear and desire compel me to possess, why not look up and around, like Kyger did? Why not be present here and now, without needing anything else?

Because, I suppose, I'm compelled by that rich old tension of possession. It's Michael, who keeps nothing, and then sticks with my mom and me for the last forty years. It's my mom's replica of Van Gogh, the singular hues in each glob. It's the copy of *This Kind* that got away.

I admire Kyger's detachment. Her poetry could be my off-ramp, my chance to set down the search. But I wasn't ready to take that exit. I needed to understand something else first—not just Kyger's wisdom about letting go, but why someone like Abe had chosen the opposite path. Why had he embraced collecting so completely? Maybe the answer wasn't in any philosophy, but in the different ways that people lived.

I decided to go back to Browsers'—this time, to find Abe.

CHAPTER 10

Browsers' Books

When I was finally ready to go back to Browsers', I left Michael behind. I needed to make this trip alone. It was too complicated, too many tangled wires of memory and books and prices and ideas about what to keep. I wasn't ready to talk to Michael about di Prima or the fact that I still thought about our copy of her book. My regret over that book felt so personal that to bring it back up would be a departure from our casual banter about how much books cost and how much they sold for. It would be worse if Michael knew I wanted to buy another copy. He would object to paying the retail price. It would make me an outsider to Michael's world, a civilian who goes out of his way to buy something just to keep.

I had expected the same meager thinking from Abe, but when I returned to his store, he betrayed none of the suspicion you found in the booksellers of Michael's generation.

"How did you get into di Prima?" I asked.

Abe paused to think. "She's just cool, you know?"

"And nobody knows her," I added.

"Exactly," Abe said.

I asked about his copy of *This Kind of Bird Flies Backward.* Abe explained that it was a reprint published by Corinth several years after the first Totem edition. Even with the same delicate paper covers, it was not the same book, not the first thing offered into the universe by Diane di Prima, practically hand printed. Abe hoped one day to purchase the original, but for now, he intended to keep the reprint as a personal copy.

He didn't need to justify how he felt. He also didn't try to sell me anything. Noting Abe's ease in his own skin, I wondered if I had missed something, if it might have been possible for me to find a place in this world after all. Abe wasn't a younger version of Michael. In him, I saw an expression of the person I might have been.

I was relieved that Abe did not possess an original copy of the book I sought, and yet I also felt another kind of longing—jealousy, maybe—of his earnest pursuit. Abe had half a shelf of di Prima's books, including her major works but also several broadsides and small-press editions, the kinds of short volumes di Prima would have given to friends to publish. I wanted to understand how Abe had acquired his interest in di Prima, the same obscure poet who was at the center of my own existential inquiry.

"You're from here?" I asked.

"I mean, I didn't grow up in this store," Abe said. "Well, I kind of did. But, like, I wasn't born inside the store."

I hadn't contemplated whether or not it was possible to be birthed by a bookstore, but Abe made me wonder.

"How did you end up here, then?"

"Oh, I needed a job," Abe said. He looked at me, saw the pleading in my eyes, took a deep breath, and then launched into the unabridged version of his life story.

The more Abe got into the details, the more our di Prima coincidence felt natural, as if we were each the perfect result of everything that had made us. He was born in the late 1990s, the year after David Foster Wallace published *Infinite Jest* and the year before I graduated high school. He was only twenty-five years old, a fact that shocked me, given that he owned his own store. He looked older, and was comfortable with himself, something I still hoped would come to me, eventually.

When Abe's father was deployed to serve in Afghanistan, his mom kept him busy by taking him to Albany's library, which was nestled among decaying residential care homes. As he was learning to read, Abe worked his way through the library's collection of books about armies and wars, scanning for pictures of airplanes and tanks, propelled by curiosity about his dad's work. As he got older, Abe was drawn toward fiction, eventually to the canon of white American authors—Hemingway, Melville, Thoreau—the serious names that impress teenage boys with a sense of importance.

Peach fuzz emerged above Abe's lip, and he started sorting his dad's books, dividing nonfiction and sci-fi onto separate shelves at home. One day he was a normal kid; the next, he needed to own every book that mattered. From a library sale here and a garage sale there, Abe assembled his own collection of tattered hardbacks, without dust jackets and most likely book club editions, of classic American novels. Eventually Abe's mom took him to Browsers' Books, the dilapidated house where the literati of Albany traded in the Nora Roberts and James Patterson novels they'd read for ones they hadn't. There, among the creased paperbacks, Abe found a two-volume, hardback set of writings by Jean-Jacques Rousseau. His frontal lobe throbbed as he made the purchase with savings from his allowance and odd jobs. *I collect, therefore I am.*

Abe would need to make money if he was going to collect books in earnest. With this impulse, he took the job available to every kid who grows up in Albany. He went down the old Highway 99E to the grass-seed farm and started bagging seed.

Humble as grass seed sounds, it's a big business, and the thin seeds, like whiskers from a shave, get into every crease in your clothing. When Abe came home from ten-hour shifts, he had seed in his hair, in his ears, around his collar, down his back and along the edges of another crease, in his pockets, and especially in the tongue and laces of his shoes. The bagging was mindless, not unpleasant, but for a person with an active brain, a tedious pursuit. You couldn't let your mind wander along the corridors of Rousseau or you would end up with somebody's lawn in your shirt pocket.

Abe was elbows-deep in seed when his cell phone had begun to ring—a high school sweetheart, idle at home, would pepper Abe's shifts with bursts of emojis and questions and ideas for the weekend. This time, she was calling about something she had seen on Facebook, a posting for a job at Browsers' Bookstore, the store up the road in Albany that Abe insisted they visit every weekend.

Abe hung up the phone, wiped the grass seed off his shirt, and drove straight up Highway 99E to Browsers'. Inside, he found the same serious, bookish-looking man who had sold Abe the Rousseau collection, sitting at a computer, surrounded by haphazardly stacked books, and looking as he always did, annoyed.

"Can I help you?"

"I'm here for the job," Abe said. He hadn't had to jump through any hoops to get hired at the farm. He just showed up.

"Do you have a resume?" the man asked.

"No," Abe said. "But I come here every weekend and I'm very organized. And I'm reading every book by Hemingway in the order he wrote them."

"What book are you on?"

"*For Whom—*," Abe said.

"*—the Bell Tolls*. You found *Torrents of Spring*?"

"That's where I started. It was the first—"

"Don't bother when you get to *Garden of Eden*," the man said. "Hemingway never wanted it published. He'd have slugged somebody if he hadn't blown his own head off."

And with that, Abe was introduced to Scott Givens, the architect of the early-2000s resurgence of Browsers' Bookstore, a man with enough business savvy to afford employees and, back then at least, the bare minimum of social grace needed to keep them. Scott looked like he'd have been at home in a bank, carefully weighing the risks of loans. Or like a high school geometry teacher perpetually disappointed by the incongruity of his students' thinking. He looked like he always needed to fart.

Since Abe had never participated in a formal job interview, he didn't think to feel caught off guard by the one that began, in earnest, with the conversation about Hemingway. Besides wanting to know what Abe was reading, Scott required Abe to answer two additional questions to prove his qualifications:

Who wrote *Moby Dick*?

What is the earth's circumference?

The first question, for Abe, was easy: Herman Melville. He hadn't read *Moby Dick*, but he owned a copy, and he was vaguely aware that the book was about much more than whale hunting. Later, under Scott's tutelage, he would commence his own quest for meaning, for possession of an understanding of the futile voyage out under the unrelenting white skies of the world. For now, the name was enough. The second question confounded Abe, but a precise answer wasn't Scott's aim. He simply needed to verify that he was hiring, from the shallow pool of otherwise qualified candidates in Albany, someone who understood the world to be round. Abe stumbled through an answer about the equator, and the number of feet in a mile, and the number of miles between Oregon and Wyoming, where his family once drove in a car, and how many times you might have to do that to circle the earth.

"No résumé, you said?" Scott asked.

"No," Abe said, "I just—"

"Don't bother," Scott said, handing Abe a dogeared bookmark from a different store. "If you want, just write your phone number on the back of this bookmark." Abe jotted down his cell phone number and handed it to Scott.

"Thanks," Scott said. He leaned back in his chair, squinting, studying Abe.

"Thanks," Abe said, standing at the counter, unsure how to proceed. "I mean, you're welcome."

"Okay," Scott said.

"Okay," said Abe.

"Okay, I'll see you later."

"Okay," said Abe. He turned and left the store.

Abe got into his car and drove back to the grass-seed farm,

thinking that his answer about the earth's circumference had been fatal to his chances. He was resigned to a career of seasonal farm labor, which at least afforded him the chance to buy used books, if not to work among them. Around midday, Abe's phone vibrated in his pocket. It was an Albany number that he didn't recognize. Abe's heart pounded.

"Abe's phone," he answered.

"Is this the Hemingway kid?" Scott didn't bother to introduce himself.

"Abe," he said.

"When do you want to start?"

"I can start right now."

"Then why aren't you here?"

"I'll be right there," Abe said. Again, he brushed the grass seed off his clothes, got in his car and drove up Highway 99E to Browsers', hopeful that he would never bag grass seed again. It turned out, Abe would learn later from Scott, that his answer about the circumference of the earth had been wildly wrong, but it had proven that Abe was willing to think his way through a problem.

Once he started at the store, Abe did everything he could to stay. He attacked the piles of books with a fervor that Scott had long since lost. When business was slow, Abe allowed himself to browse among shelves, to check publication pages and skim the beginnings and endings of the books that made him curious. He took all the afternoon and weekend shifts until he finished high school. When he started at the local community college, he shuttled between the store and campus as his coursework required.

Between shifts and homework assignments, Abe began reading from some academic's list of books that comprise the Western canon, from Homer to James Joyce. Though limited to a narrow and unrepresentative view, that of mostly white men who wrote before the twenty-first century, it was a journey with books that, even if it took years, Abe could complete. It was reading, and at the same time, it was collecting.

There was also the matter of Abe's formal education, which he pursued at Linn-Benton Community College—on Highway 99E between the grass-seed farm and Browsers'. There, he staked out his identity as an intellectual by carrying around a copy of *Infinite Jest*. The book must've weighed ten pounds.

He liked his community-college writing class so much that when it was offered again with the same instructor, he took it a second time. The instructor cooked up a mutually beneficial arrangement in which Abe registered for the class, thereby ensuring enough students that the class would not be canceled, and then was allowed to withdraw so that he would not have to pay tuition.

It was in this audit, this time an evening class, that Abe met the person who would, a couple of years later, become his wife. In the writing class, another student shared a story about an obsessive woman who wanted to live inside a man's body. Afterward, Abe offered her his copy of *Infinite Jest*, promising, if she read it, that she might see what it was like to live inside of him. She returned the book after about a month. "I tried," she told Abe. For Abe, the effort was enough. They began to meet up and discuss literature, and after a short while, to meet up with no need to discuss anything at all. Not long after, they would marry.

When Abe had earned enough transfer credits, he enrolled at Oregon State University to work toward his four-year degree. He had hoped to find instructors and students who believed the world to be as expansive and full of ideas as he had found it. In some cases, such as in his nonfiction writing class with Justin St. Germain, he felt at home, even if his peers weren't quite sure what to make of Abe's prose, which was less than linear. When Abe submitted an abstract essay based on the work of the architect Le Corbusier, St. Germain, the instructor, told Abe, "I don't know what to do with this, but it's cool. Keep doing it."

But the rest of his education at Oregon State University fell short of community college. At Linn-Benton, Abe found faculty committed to teaching. In return, he was excited to learn. At Oregon State, most students and instructors were jumping through the transactional hoops of grades and scholarship. Where Abe had hoped to find his own dead poets' society, he found instead a treadmill of banal ambition, a pathway for kids from Portland suburbs to preserve their middle-class status. Abe noticed what other students knew intuitively: that success on society's terms had little to do with learning.

The whole time he studied, from high school to community college to completing his four-year degree, Abe worked at Browsers', earning the education that would define him. Scott would ask Abe questions about his interests and point him to books, giving Abe the chance to cultivate his own curiosity about obscure strains of human knowledge, tracing the progress of ideas as he shelved books.

Working in a bookstore is a way to map the world, like a liberal arts degree. You get a sense of what's out there by studying each book in a section. You go deeper where your curiosity takes you, but you're also able to see how a breadth of understanding is possible across disciplines, subjects. You could see how Abe's time in community college and at Browsers' meant more than a transactional experience at a four-year institution.

After graduating, Abe continued at Browsers', working full time with increasing responsibilities. He suggested changes, like organizing colorful displays of books, that were well received by customers. He was well liked by the older employees, such as Gerry Rouff, who had been around bookstores their entire lives. Abe was a different creature because of his youth, but anyone who loved books would see a kindred spirit in him.

Everything changed in 2021, when Scott called all of his various full- and part-time employees—surly, bookish types who were immediately suspicious—into a meeting before the store's open hours. This had never happened, that anyone could recall, in the store's two decades of operations. Gerry, who was working only one day a week by that time, drifted in. Scott cleared his throat and spoke directly, which was his manner, telling the employees that the store would be listed for sale, not because there was any problem with the business, but because he was making a personal transition and needed to move away from the store. Employees soon surmised, correctly, that Scott and his wife were working through a divorce and that the store, as a matter of marital property, could not be easily divided between the parties. Scott would have to convert his interest in the store into some kind of reducible asset, and the easiest way to do this was to sell it. In an attempt to lighten the mood of the meeting, Abe joked, "I'll take it."

Browsers' was well known in Albany and had a devoted base of customers. Several potential buyers inquired about the store, and despite its volume of sales, found it impossible to secure financing from a bank. Even Abe met with a local banker to ask about the possibility of a loan. Inevitably, the bank would sniff out the financial precariousness that lingered around booksellers.

After failing to find a buyer to secure an interest in the store, Scott circled back to Abe.

"Were you serious when you said you would take the store?"

Abe was deadly serious. He wanted nothing more than to stay at Browsers'. With no other buyer, Scott figured he could hold a sale to liquidate enough of his stock to buy out his wife, while keeping the building and renting it back to Abe, who would start out with whatever books remained. This would allow the store and the goodwill it had built to carry forward.

While Abe never flinched at the possibility of living his dream, he was aware of its risks. "How does this fail?" he asked Scott.

"Robots," Scott said.

Scott explained that the store might fail, but if so, it would be for reasons they could not yet foresee. It would be a new technology, a shift in the market for used books, or another pandemic. It would not fail for lack of effort, as Abe had already worked hard for six years at Browsers'. He knew what it would take to survive.

To help Abe take over the store, his family, including his grandparents, came to join him in revamping the old rambler full of books. Ferrying back and forth to a big-box hardware store down the street, and with a gusher of elbow grease, the family transformed the interior of the rundown home into a proper bookstore.

❧

I realized that Abe and I had been talking for an hour as he freely offered me his story and that I, despite always being conscious of time, of not imposing, had lost myself in his words. As I began to feel embarrassed for lingering with Abe for so long, the bell on the bookstore's door clanged and a familiar face appeared. I recognized the easy smile and tousled gray hair of Michael's old friend, Gerry Rouff. I knew that Gerry had worked at Browsers' when Scott owned it, and Abe had mentioned Gerry several times, but still, I was surprised by the coincidence. And then I recalled how Gerry turned up everywhere we went.

Except that this time, in this context, I could see in his expression, after he greeted Abe, that he didn't remember me.

"Gerry, it's me, Danny. Michael's stepson."

"Oh, Danny," Gerry said. "You still reading Burroughs?"

Of course he remembered.

I stammered a reply. The scene was surreal. Whereas I had cast off everything Michael had taught me and willed myself away from a life in books, Abe had allowed his dream, owning a bookstore, to come to him. Michael's old friend had drifted in, and there was a shelf full of di Prima's books. Even if his copy of *This Kind* was a reprint, Abe was running the bookstore of my dreams in between strip malls in Albany, Oregon.

CHAPTER 11

Serendipity

Since Abe didn't have an original copy of *This Kind of Bird Flies Backward*, and I wasn't willing to talk to Michael about it, there was only one other person I knew who might help me: Gerry Rouff. Gerry had been around when I first became interested in Beat poetry. He worked at Browsers' Bookstore for Scott and lingered after Abe took over. He remains, among booksellers, the person who is friends with everyone, who buys something at every store he visits, who remembers what matters to people.

When I saw Gerry at Browsers', he was dropping in to sell Abe a handful of books he'd found at other stores—books he'd picked out specifically for Abe, buying them at dealer prices to resell at a modest profit. To sweeten the deal, Gerry brought another book or two from his collection to give to Abe as a gift. At our chance encounter at Browsers', he'd given me the business card for his one-man operation, Studio Books. It listed his phone number and an address in Corvallis.

Dialing Gerry's number on my phone felt strange. Every time I'd ever seen him, he'd just happened to turn up. Now that I needed help to find di Prima, I would have to reach out proactively. I wasn't sure if this was how book scouts would normally interact.

"Hello," Gerry answered.

"Hi, Gerry. This is Danny." Michael was one of the last people who used the diminutive of my name. It was how Gerry would know me.

"Oh, Danny," he said, drawing out my name, warmly. I knew immediately he was happy for the call. I took a deep breath and proceeded as best I knew how in this new landscape.

"I'm starting to get back into books," I said. "I was thinking, maybe we could—"

"Sure," Gerry said, cutting to it. He must have sensed I needed help. "Why don't you come over to my place? I can show you some books and we can talk more."

I agreed and we set a date. Gerry then described every turn I'd make between my home and Eugene and his in Corvallis, directions that I jotted down and then promptly discarded, knowing I'd use the map in my phone.

On the appointed date, I arrived at a small house in the Southtown part of Corvallis, where the orderly college town gave way to its agricultural roots. At the address Gerry gave, I detected a designer's touch in the choice of colors in the trim, and in the arrangement of objects around the garden out front. Could this, I wondered, be Gerry?

When I knocked on his door, I heard from inside the house the swift movement of someone who has been waiting for company, eager for a visit. Gerry opened the door, smiling, and welcomed me in. "Coffee?" he asked.

Looking back, I'm sure I heard Gerry, but in my preoccupation with di Prima, and in this new context for my relationship with Gerry, all I could do was scan his bookshelves. Did he have a copy of the book I was looking for? Had he ever had one? What had happened to one that got away from us? Every second that passed took me back a year, and before Gerry's question registered, it was the turn of the century, around when Michael had found the di Prima.

"Coffee?" Gerry asked again.

"No," I said abruptly. And then came the regret. Of course I wanted coffee. I would need it if I was going to keep up with Gerry's banter. But it was too late.

Out on the table where I'd sat and where Gerry settled in with his coffee, I noticed an old literary journal, something I didn't recognize, with a squiggly pencil illustration on the cover so goofy that it could only have been printed in the 1970s. I looked more closely at the cover, and what I saw gave me a chill: Diane di Prima was listed among the contributors. What was this book doing here? Abe's interest in di Prima could be explained by coincidence; this could not.

There was something about Gerry, or maybe about myself, that I hadn't considered. He was always thoughtful, always had a kind word. Because he was always present, I'd never examined my feelings about him. As I sat at his coffee table, carefully weighing my options, coffee or no coffee, I realized that I didn't entirely trust Gerry.

"How's the book business?" I asked. This question may sound innocuous, but it was a power move and we both knew it. The pressure was back on Gerry, who would have to answer the question artfully, since we both know the truth.

"If the book business was any good, I wouldn't be the last one in it," he said. It had the ring of truth.

"Why do you do it, then?" And then, feeling overly harsh, "I mean, how did you get into the business?"

Gerry took a long draw off his coffee. He told me how he'd grown up in a middle-class family in Los Angeles, with Russian Jewish roots, and attended UCLA. Assigned a high draft number during the Vietnam War, he enrolled in a PhD program for history and took a side job at a textbook store. He liked the bookstore more than he'd ever liked school, and eventually, Gerry left the graduate program and began working at stores in Beverly Hills and Santa Monica. Back then, salespeople would come in with new books. Gerry was tasked with ordering paperbacks from their catalogs. It was the same business model, Gerry explained, that bookstores had used since the nineteenth century.

Hanging around the bookstores, Gerry was exposed to writers he hadn't read before, such as Thomas Pynchon and William Gaddis.

The other salespeople fashioned themselves as bohemians, smoking cigarettes and going out for drinks after work. They turned Gerry on to the poet W. S. Merwin and derided the early success of Stephen King. In the art book section of the store where Gerry worked, there was an older saleswoman who took Gerry under her wing. She had previously worked at a high-end shop in Santa Monica and had cultivated her own list of book-buying clients. This, Gerry said, was his real education. It occurred to me that book scouts, Gerry among them, had been part of my education also.

Gerry traveled from California to live in Amsterdam, but before he left, he sold his book collection to a dealer in Berkeley named Peter Howard. Peter, who ran Serendipity Books, was well known among the booksellers of his time. He made book-buying trips across the United States and Europe and connected with sellers and buyers wherever he went. If Peter had never seen a book before, Gerry said, he was sure to buy it. Serendipity's catalogs covered so much of the market for modern literature that other dealers would use them as price guides. Peter also cultivated top-shelf clients to buy his books. If the right client was interested in a particular author, he would buy everything he could find, Gerry said, with an almost clinical disinterest in the books themselves. When Gerry visited Peter's house, he didn't see a single book.

Gerry became animated as he spoke about Peter. He jumped up from his chair and, in the same frenetic motion, pulled a hardback copy of *A Gentle Madness* down from his shelf. This was Nicholas Basbanes's book about rich and neurotic book collectors, published in the 1990s—a signpost that there may have been a lucrative career ahead of Gerry and even Michael. Gerry opened the book straight to page 283, where a crease must have formed in the book's spine, because there, Basbanes discusses Peter Howard's business selling every American novel ever written to Carter Burden, a lawyer and heir to the Vanderbilt fortune. It was the stuff of legend, and to Peter's own telling, it was the birth of the market for modern first editions. Whatever Peter's actual place in the pantheon of booksellers, his appearance in Basbanes's book clearly meant something to Gerry.

While Gerry was in Europe, he scouted books and sent them back to Peter to sell at Serendipity. Gerry returned after a year and worked with Peter at the store. Finally, fed up with small apartments and the saturated used-book scene in Berkeley, Gerry settled in Oregon, where he had a brother. It was here that Gerry first met Michael at his store in Salem—though he visited only once, searching for obscure novels in translation, the kind of books that didn't routinely pass through Michael's hands.

"Did you think it was a decent store?" I asked. I wanted him to tell me that Michael had been good at what he did.

"It was a typical bookstore," Gerry said. "You have to be crazy to open a store. All bookstores are run by crazy people."

Gerry knew what he was talking about. He'd picked up shifts at the Book Bin, hung around Michael's attempt at a store in Corvallis, and then worked for Scott Givens at Browsers'. I wondered whether he had his own dream of opening a store. He'd always had the books for it. Perhaps Gerry's wife, an artist and curator whose day job paid for their charming house, discouraged him. Gerry was less inclined toward misery than most scouts. He may have been missing a gene.

We talked about the internet. Unlike every other scout I knew, Gerry didn't lament the internet, blaming it for slow business. He understood that the book business had never been good to begin with, and that the internet hurt only those dealers who couldn't adapt. For those who had, the internet could be very good for the business of bookselling. The problem was that it changed the shape of the enterprise from something a person could do, relying on wit alone, to a volume business requiring employees, scanners, and if you're successful, a warehouse. Nobody needed another used bookstore.

Which is how we got to talking about Abe.

"What he's doing is great," Gerry said.

I parsed Gerry's words. He didn't say, "he's doing great." Certainly not, "business is great." What Gerry had offered was tempered, distanced from himself. What he was saying was, *I'm glad Abe has his store because it's a place where I can go and engage in a series of small transactions that are slightly beneficial to me, while keeping up on whatever gossip Abe has access to.* What he wanted to say was, *Only an idiot would try to run a bookstore.* Against my own loyalties, I agreed with Gerry on this point.

My curiosity returned to the journal on the table, containing some work by di Prima. It sat directly between us, agonizingly. Why did he have this book? Why had he set it out? Gerry caught my eyes on the journal but said nothing.

"Shall we go see Abe?" he asked.

"Now?" I asked, feeling like we had unfinished business.

"Why not?" he said.

"Sure," I said. I didn't know what Gerry was up to, but I wanted to see how it would unfold. "I can't take you in the Prius," I added. "I have to go to work after Browsers."

"No problem," Gerry said, collecting the di Prima from the table and motioning me toward the front door. "I've got the Toyota."

In the driveway sat Gerry's car—a collection of rusted aluminum, bald tires, and cracked glass old enough to be Kerouac's ride in *On the Road*. Though Gerry called it a Toyota, it had transcended make and model to become something more essential: a vehicle perfectly evolved to travel from Corvallis to Albany and, if luck held, back again.

I got into the Prius and as the engine began its soft, melodic hum, I had time to consider, without distraction, what Gerry was doing with the di Prima. That he had set it out in front of me was no accident, nor was the fact that he hadn't mentioned it. There were no coincidences in this business. He may have been waiting for me to ask, but I wasn't about to walk into that trap.

It turned out that Gerry had a bigger plan—to go and visit Abe in Albany. He must have sorted through the probabilities—whether I would ask about the book, and perhaps make a handsome offer for it, and if not, the likelihood of a bidding war between Abe and me once we got to Browsers'. Gerry wasn't particularly venal, but he was clever. If that book got to Albany before me, I'd have to contend with Abe if I wanted it.

The rumble of Gerry's engine smothered the hum of the Prius. He was already on the move, his car lurching through the back streets of south Corvallis, hardly stopping to take right turns. Gerry had been trained in the streets of California, where he was not beholden to Oregon's culture of passive driving. My handler had been Michael, who puttered along in the slow lane, leveraging his patience for deception. I would have to blow my cover to beat Gerry this time. At least, that's how it seemed to my over-caffeinated, di Prima-obsessed brain.

Once I got the Prius out of the back streets, I saw Gerry ahead of me, advancing on the ramp to the state highway that would take us to Albany. I gunned it—if you can call it that in a Prius—pressing the pedal all the way down until the speedometer heroically ticked up past ten, twenty, thirty miles an hour. By the time we got onto Highway 34, I'd gathered some momentum and was finally able to overtake Gerry in his jalopy. He didn't look over as I passed him, his eyes locked onto the road ahead.

The turn to Albany is a left across two lanes of highway traffic, so I rolled the dice and shot in front of a truck. Sure as shit, Gerry did too, showing no concern for his own life as he made his pursuit. By then I had dropped my phone on the floor and would have to make the last few turns to Browsers' by memory.

There's a shortcut, if you can remember it: instead of looping all the way around Albany's chaotic street plan, you can cut through the parking lot of the drugstore. And I did. But Gerry, who had made this drive a thousand times, cut through the fast-food lot instead, shaving fifteen seconds off the trip and pulling up at Browsers' Bookstore a split second before me. He was out of his car before it had stopped running, and by the time I was inside, he was already negotiating a price for the di Prima with Abe.

CHAPTER 12

Passages

I knew from searching for books with Michael that most of the time, you didn't find much, and if you did, it usually wasn't what you were looking for. I wanted to keep talking to Abe, to know whether he got the same dull ache in his gut when looking for di Prima that I felt when I saw her books. I wanted to know whether my search could be a little bit less singular. I wanted to be Abe's friend.

From my own perch—middle age—it's not easy to make friends. There are the ones I've clung to since high school and college, now more desperately than ever, aware of the social abyss surrounding men of my age. There are the parents of my children's friends, men like me with thinning hair and expressions of exasperation as they push their children on swings at the playground. There are colleagues in my office whose company I enjoy, though the invisible cell doors of our bureaucracy will never breach. I had no friends who, like me, wanted to look for used books.

Abe, I thought, would be the kind of friend who would understand the way I scoured a thrift store or worked the poetry section at a store, scanning for authors of note and checking small-press folios for the rare gem. He knew the science of checking the publications page to confirm a first edition, and the thrill of discovering an overlooked signature. I wouldn't have to worry with Abe about the excitement I felt when I found a book worth several times what

I'd paid. To our thinking, that was the point. And so, anxious to secure his friendship, I emailed Abe.

Hi Abe,
Wondering, is there a day when we might head up to Portland to check around for some di Primas? Would be fun to make the trip together and see some interesting books. I'm happy to drive if it's helpful. Let me know what you think.
Daniel

After sending the email, I wondered about the wisdom of proposing a day trip to another bookseller. Why would he want to drive around looking for books with a customer? Days went by with no reply. I wondered if I should retract my offer and retreat, friendless. Then came Abe's response:

Hey!
I'm sorry for the slow reply. There's lots to catch up on despite being here most days . . .
Any Monday would work great for me. I'll ask if Gerry wants to come. I don't have a car, so if one of you could drive that would be excellent. Otherwise, I'm up for anything.
Abe

Whew. I read it once quickly for the answer and then again to absorb nuance, for any hint that he'd been less than interested in going. I found only enthusiasm. The surprise was that we would bring Gerry, though it was never surprising any more when he turned up. Knowing the way old scouts stay in touch, it would definitely get back to Michael that we'd gone looking for di Prima. I suspected it was also necessary: Gerry would know where to find what we were looking for.

On the appointed Monday, I skidded across puddles in my Prius until I found Gerry and Abe at Browsers', where we had agreed to meet before I drove us all up to Portland. Both of their faces appeared in the window; they had been watching, waiting for me. They were excited.

On the drive up, Gerry took the front seat, maybe due to age and custom, or maybe Abe deferred, knowing as well as I did that Gerry was the only one of us capable of sustaining an hour of conversation.

"Have you ever seen David's books at Passages?" Gerry asked. I detected the slyness in Gerry's framing, anticipating that he'd be the only one in the car connected enough to answer in the affirmative.

"Who?" I'm too old to play games, I thought.

"David. He runs Passages. We can go see his books."

Some dealers have a bookstore; others have a storage space; and others, like Gerry, have something in between: a house or a studio or maybe a garage where they keep their books. On this mission, it was our objective to figure out where this person called David kept his books.

"Where do we find David?" I asked, avoiding any presumption.

"Oh, David's got his place in Northwest Portland. Passages. He's got some old *Floating Bears*. You'll like his place."

Gerry was being cagy. I didn't care whether David sold his books out of a pigeon coop or a penthouse above Powell's, but Gerry had not let this information trickle out casually. Before the trip, Gerry would have reached back deep into the recesses of his memory, and may have even worked the phones, to find out who among the Portland scouts might possess di Prima. If Gerry said we would be interested, there was a strong possibility of finding something rare, exquisite.

The *Floating Bear* was certainly that. Like the caviar of collectible Beat ephemera, it was the newsletter published by di Prima and Baraka and then distributed through the US Postal Service to a small readership that included the talented writers and poets of the Beat Generation. Nearly forty volumes had been published, the first in runs of only a few dozen copies. Each specimen of the newsletter had been handled, stapled, and posted by di Prima herself. The mention of the *Floating Bear* was a lure set out by an intrepid dealer, baited by Gerry, and dropped in front of me, glimmering.

As I merged onto I-5, Gerry held court, telling us about a scouting trip he'd made in the seventies with Peter Howard. I thought of the three of us—Gerry, myself, and Abe—and how we each represented a different generation on this journey. The stories that Gerry passed down, whether intended or not, might contain information that Abe would find useful to survive in the business. For myself, I wasn't sure what to do with Gerry's stories about Serendipity—whether to gather them up with follow-up questions or to leave them on the shelves in the thrift store of my memory. Abe and I mostly left Gerry's stories undisturbed.

The subject turned to the book club that Abe was starting, which consisted of a handful of old Browsers' employees, two customers who like the same kinds of books that Abe does, and two customers who offered to join just to support Abe. The theme of the book club was that it would only read books that were difficult. Whether he meant difficult to read or to enjoy, I wasn't sure. The idea, he explained, was to build a community around thousand-page tomes of experimental fiction from the mid-twentieth century. Books would be selected either by Abe or one of his misanthropic friends on the bases of length, obscurity, and lack of appeal. For its first book, the club would read a 956-page book by postmodern writer William Gaddis called *The Recognitions,* whose notoriety peaked in 2002 when Jonathan Franzen called it the most difficult book he'd ever read.

For his part, Gerry had no qualms about reading *The Recognitions.* In fact, he salivated at the chance that he might select a book for the club so that he too could impart some misery. His own choice would be a novel by the experimental Austrian author Walter Abish, who was famous, according to Gerry, for interspersing the perspectives of different characters so seamlessly that it was impossible to know, at any point, who was telling the story.

They agreed that the book club would inevitably read David Foster Wallace. How could it not? If a club was formed for the purpose of reading difficult, unpleasant fiction, how could it ignore the genre's star? Abe had already polled the book club's members and determined that none wanted to read *Infinite Jest*, which, in addition to the novel's interminable length and lack of focus, would make it a perfect selection for the club.

As we discussed obscure and difficult novels that Abe and Gerry agreed were as unappreciated now as ever, I realized that I am different from them not only in my desire to own books but also in the way I read. I like books with stories in them. The story need not be neat and tidy, nor particularly easy to absorb, but I prefer writing that introduces me to characters I come to care about and then shows me what happens to them.

The three of us barreled north on I-5, crossing under the tram line and into Portland, where the first of many small decisions demanded our attention. In my mind's eye, we'd take a precise route to the interstate exit, where we'd be delivered almost directly to David Abel's place at an address Gerry gave in Northwest Portland. But as the freeway forked, Gerry insisted we would find our way more easily by traveling through the city. I deferred to his wisdom, which led us down Naito Parkway and across a landscape of makeshift villages of tents and tarps, their inhabitants emerging occasionally to lurch toward the street, causing momentary panic among drivers like me who were less accustomed to the challenges of urban circumnavigation. We followed the parkway past the bridges until the Pearl District rose before us, its impersonal glass and steel now two decades old, a playground for people who design computer chips and subsist on macronutrient smoothies.

As we reached the outer enclaves of the Pearl District, I noticed that the traffic signals had gone dark, and then, ominously, that the lights in the buildings and their storefronts were out also. Gerry and Abe seemed anxious, giving competing suggestions for parking places. Passages Bookshop, Gerry indicated, was on the sixth floor of a converted factory building. It was a wobbling brick fortress distinct enough from its surroundings to suggest the old Portland, back before *Portlandia* and the Ace Hotel and even before La Luna. Before Walt Curtis wrote *Mala Noche* and Gus Van Sant made it into a movie. A literal tower of bricks, the building did not appear as though it had been engineered to endure, and yet, it had.

When we got to the entrance, the intercom was out, dimming our scouting prospects until a stranger let us in a side door to a dark stairwell.

"All the way up to six," Gerry said, and although he had a three-decade advantage over me and nearly five on Abe, he led the charge. After climbing the dark stairwell, we entered the main area of the sixth floor, finding a labyrinth of studio spaces and offices dedicated to the business of Portland's fringe industries, or maybe its main ones: film, massage, printmaking. Gerry led us down one hall, then back, then down another hallway across from the first one. Finally, we found ourselves outside of a locked door at the end of a dark hallway, where there was a cart of books marked 50 percent off. Abe used the flashlight on his phone to read the sign on the door: *Passages Bookshop*. With the door locked and no obvious next step, I fired up my phone's flashlight and began to scout the rolling cart of discount books. Nothing interested me, but I watched Abe snap up a handful of nineteenth-century British novels and the journal of a pioneer settler in the Midwestern United States.

We heard footsteps down the hall and, in that instant, my heartbeat quickened, if not because of the horror film scenario we'd found ourselves in, then at the thought of meeting the dealer who, as Gerry had mentioned, may be in possession of some old *Floating Bears*. Not only that, but I wondered about the kind of person who would deal in the kinds of books I longed for, whether we would connect over our uncommon pursuit, as I had with Abe.

Finally, David arrived.

As David advanced toward us up the dark corridor, I noticed first his height, and then his deliberate gait. The book dealers I had known were crouched, feeble men, perhaps molded by their intrepid genes or by years of contortion to fit into the nooks and cracks in the universe where treasures can be found. David was not like this; he was tall and composed, elegant for a dealer and, you might think if you were to see him in the street, normal.

When Abe and I turned our flashlights toward him, and he greeted us with a smile and a hello, I noticed that his whiskers, unlike all the other dealers who kept them, were trimmed down, shaped into a goatee, not allowed to roam free down across his lips, collecting seeds and crumbs and whatever else it was that Michael's mustache trapped. David had dark, curly hair and looked sharp in his jacket and jeans that fit him. He didn't look like any book scout I'd ever met before.

As soon as David had unlocked the door, we began rifling through books, still in the dark. We used the hint of light from the windows, along with our phones, to scan the scene like burglars. Abe found the fiction section, and I installed myself between him and the shelves of poetry, where I hoped a volume or two of di Prima might be discovered. In the darkness, David was somewhere watching us as we pawed through his collection.

Abe dispatched quickly with fiction, gathering a handful of unreadable novels. Then he stalked the glass case where David kept his better books. Not wanting Abe to beat me to the good stuff, I left poetry and followed Abe over, tapping his shoulder lightly to let him know I was there. I was ready to snatch *This Kind* from the shelf in front of him if needed.

Our heads nearly touched as we huddled over the "D" section in the case, studying titles between a clump of Carvers and all the various Ginsbergs. I spotted it first: *Loba as Eve II*, one of di Prima's rarest books, printed on onionskin paper, bound in hard covers, and signed and limited to fifty numbered copies. It was on sale for $600. This volume was one of the few collectible books I still owned, bought from a catalog back in the 1990s. Abe used his phone to look up the price of the book and then calculate the price with the discount he'd get from David. I could tell by the pain in his eyes that it was out of reach. In that instant, I wanted to give Abe my copy of the book, knowing what it meant to him. And at the same time, I wanted to buy a second copy for myself so that no one else could possess it. I could track down all fifty copies.

"Hey guys," David called across the store. "Come over here when you're ready."

Abe was ready, materializing next to David at the counter while I lurked at the glass case. I was trying to examine a two-volume set by William Stafford, and as I lifted the case containing the set from the shelf, one of the books leapt out, nearly falling to the floor below, except that, with just enough of the scout's adrenaline in my own veins, my free hand darted down and caught the book. Mercifully, no one had noticed, and I nestled the pristine set, marked at $300, back on the shelf inside the case.

On the other side of the store, I found Abe and David joined by Gerry, the three of them shoulder to shoulder over David's counter. Standing on the tips of my toes and peering over from the far end of the counter, I observed, in David's hands, a letter-sized steel box, like a safe-deposit box you would see in the movies. David removed a lid and produced, as we watched breathlessly in the dark, a nearly complete set of all thirty-seven issues of the *Floating Bear*, missing only issues two and three. Those, he explained, are nearly impossible to find. Then, from a second steel box set out on the counter, David removed and handed to Abe a handful of spare issues of the *Floating Bear*, duplicates of the ones in the set but in worse condition. In addition to the nearly complete set and the duplicate copies, David pointed to several issues of the *Floating Bear* originally mailed by di Prima to the artist Jasper Johns, who was among the small group of people who received the publication in their mailbox. Johns's New York address was printed on each issue, likely in di Prima's hand.

Since the *Floating Bear* was distributed only by mail, you knew who each specimen had been sent to. When they occasionally made their way to market, their price was set by the condition of the newsletter, the earliness of the volume, and the name of the recipient to whom the particular volume of the newsletter was addressed. Among the addresses available to collect were names of people who had disappeared into the chaos of the sixties, or the boredom of normal life. But many, like Johns, became famous poets and painters of their generations.

David handled the mimeographs casually. They were far from the rarest books he'd touch on any given day. They'd been around and changed hands often in the course of his career and would again, he knew. David offered Abe duplicates to buy. Abe, as a fellow dealer, would have the right of first refusal before I would, and he would also be afforded a 20 percent discount.

Abe wanted those *Floating Bears*, I knew, but the price would cut into any savings he'd managed to accumulate from his sales at Browsers'. In this instant I saw exasperation in Abe's face, a recognition that his choices would have consequences. They would cost nearly $500, a small fortune for a bookseller. Abe was pursuing a line of business that didn't pencil out, and he knew it. It was not a choice Michael would have allowed himself to make.

Abe set five duplicate issues of the *Floating Bear* aside in a neat pile. They were later volumes of the newsletter, from the late sixties and early seventies, and they had not been sent to anyone notable. But it didn't matter; such was the compulsion to possess them all, eventually. There was another, more forlorn, coffee-stained volume that Abe didn't want. This scrap, cast aside by the dealers, was the only di Prima I would have the chance to own that day. I picked it up for myself.

With his di Primas secured on the counter by an unspoken understanding that he would continue to scout and then pay a lump sum for everything he found, Abe returned to the stacks and continued to amass a small collection of obscure novels. Having exhausted the poetry section, I clutched my lone, battered volume of the *Floating Bear*, too anxious to set it down even though it had been passed over. I began circling the store, unable to focus on the books, looking instead for meaning in the physical space and then in the people around me. David told Gerry about handmade books he'd bought from street artists in Mexico and Cuba, that he could resell to university collections at handsome prices. He dropped the names of other scouts and dealers, writers and collectors, people of note who had graced his store or otherwise been involved in one side or another of a transaction.

As David described the world of collectors and dealers, I thought: *This web is much bigger than I'd known. Most everyone in it knows more than I ever will about di Prima or anyone else.* Michael was a part of this world, but in the way that David described it, Michael felt smaller. Worse, you could get tangled up in the web as a collector, the fool in every story.

The protagonist was always the astute bookman. Peter Howard of Serendipity Books was one such hero. Or Scott Brown, a Portland dealer whose name I'd heard, but with just enough context to confuse him with Scott Givens. Scott Givens would eventually become a kind of protagonist in my own search, though I didn't know it then. At Passages Bookshop, I was a lowly collector, a mark whose lack of sophistication provided for the real scouts' enrichment.

And then the lights came on. The gloom of my internal monologue abated, giving way to a kind of clarity. I looked around and found myself inside a private bookstore, a space that was clean and bright with views across Northwest Portland, with comfortable chairs to welcome guests, with open spaces and no clutter. I'd never been in such a space. It must have surprised Abe also, because he quickly returned to the counter to finish his business with David.

As David tallied the price, Abe clenched his jaw, desperate to possess his copies of the *Floating Bear*. David mercifully applied a discount on top of the prices he'd quoted. Gerry was all smiles—happy for Abe and that David had come through.

David looked at me conspiratorially. "Want to see something?" he asked.

I didn't, really. But it wasn't really a question.

He led me to a back room where he kept, apparently, the books that were unavailable to the general public. Gerry followed us.

"Look at this," David said, removing an inauspicious hardback from the shelf and opening to its title page. David held the book out for me to examine. I understood that I was not to take possession with my own hands.

It was Mary Oliver's first book. The title page was inscribed by the author to her own mother on Christmas, before the book was even published.

"Wow," I said, sincerely. "What is something like this worth?"

David closed the book and set it back on the shelf.

"If you have to ask, you can't afford it," Gerry said.

Back in the bright room with three scouts buzzing from their transactions, it was clear to me that I wasn't one of them. Even though I sensed Abe's relief to possess the *Floating Bears,* I felt more satisfied knowing that whatever money I didn't spend on books would grow with compound interest. I also didn't care, in the way that David and Gerry did, about who had a store back when and who they knew and what kinds of books they'd discovered and held onto and eventually let go of and for how much. The fate of booksellers was stressful for me to think about. I knew the stakes of unpaid rent and the strange meals you have to cobble together when you strike out at the buyer's table. And worse, by the pain in Abe's eyes as he laid down a card to pay for his books, I saw that the pursuit had the potential to hurt him—not only that he might run out of money and have to close his store, but that, in the final tally, he would inevitably fall a volume or two short, would never complete the set. He would have to sell it all anyway, as Michael did.

I set the coffee-stained copy of the *Floating Bear* back on the counter where I'd found it. I didn't want it. Not to own, not to say I had one, not just for the thrill of possessing something that we all knew would disappear eventually into university libraries, driving its price ever higher. I couldn't stand the gnawing feeling in my stomach that it caused, that seemed to propel these people forward.

Gerry bought a stack of books, God knows what. "You gotta buy stuff to keep the whole thing going," he said. He was at ease with himself and the universe. He had figured out not only how to continue to exist in this ecosystem but how to help sustain it.

Still needing to buy something, I reached for the table next to the counter, where I found two stacks of new books for sale, offered like candy in the checkout aisle for the kind of impulsive purchase I was about to make. My choices included a small press run of David's own poetry, and an expensive book of prints by Salem artist D. E. May, distributed by a gallery run by a friend of David's. As skeptical as I was of the idea that Salem produced worthwhile visual art, I could not bring myself to give David money for his own book, and so I chose the prints.

I was relieved, when I paid for the book, that David had not seen fit to offer me the discount that he'd applied to Abe's *Floating Bears*.

CHAPTER 13

Friendship

After Portland, my obsession with *This Kind* quieted, as did my worry about my aging parents. Instead, I fretted over Abe's binge at Passages. Those volumes of the *Floating Bear* would have cost about a month of Browsers' profits. I found in my stomach the same pit planted by a lifetime of exposure to Michael's precarious enterprise.

Despite everything I knew about the business, I longed to know more about Abe—to know how he felt about our experience in Portland. I wanted to know if he was as excited about the *Floating Bear* as he had been before he'd spent the money. What I really wanted to know was whether he'd had fun, and whether the friendship I thought I was beginning to feel was reciprocal.

This time, I didn't have to labor over another email to Abe, because he wrote to me. He'd found something of interest related to di Prima that he wanted me to see. When I got to Abe's store, he presented me with *The Catalog of the Diane di Prima Occult Library*. With sparkling gold font and an etching of a lion on card stock, bound by the kind of spiral they do at Kinko's, it wasn't clear if it was a catalog or a book. Something about its rough beauty reminded me of di Prima herself. On the back page, the publisher was identified as TKS Books, and the edition was numbered—number thirty-five of fifty-five copies. The publisher presumed that it would one day be valuable.

An introduction was provided by a certain M. C. Kinniburgh, but no other author or editor is identifiable, adding to the intrigue. I flipped through the pages, listing titles from di Prima's shelves on what she had called "magick"—witchcraft, astral projection, various hallucinogens. The books themselves had been sold to the University of North Carolina. I wondered what scholars in Chapel Hill intended to do with di Prima's annotations on alchemy. For that matter, what was I supposed to do with the catalog?

"It's for you," Abe said.

"Great," I said. "How much?"

"Oh, nothing," he said. "I got another one for myself. Just something for you to have."

It occurred to me that what Abe had given me was a gift. He found something that interested him, decided it would please me also, and spent money to buy me something I hadn't asked for. This single act eclipsed the thoughtfulness of most any gesture from Michael, who had taken to giving me remainders of Barry Lopez—a writer we both disliked—for Christmas. Abe's generosity moved me.

He told me about another book he was considering buying for himself, a bootlegged copy of di Prima's best-known work, *Revolutionary Letters*. Given that she never appeared on any bestseller lists, it was probably di Prima herself, or someone she was close to, who fired up the press without concern for what City Lights might say. In di Prima's life in the sixties, she meant for her work to be read, not to collect dust on bookstore shelves. And she probably needed money. I was careful not to pressure Abe to spend another hundred dollars. No university library would care to own a bootlegged copy, and it would be difficult to establish its market value. I knew that Abe, however, would still want it. He would contemplate two future versions of his life: the one with the di Prima and the one without.

After Abe's gesture, I felt the instinct to do something that would be unthinkable among the well-mannered families we knew in Eugene: to drop in. It helped that Browsers' was open to the public, but I also knew that to visit a bookman in his place of business is what it means to be friends in this world. Michael's ill-ease in anyone else's bookstore had taught me that such visits were intimate, traveling close to someone else's life's work.

I tried not to overthink it. After work, with a box of books in my Prius that I'd hoped to give to Abe to resell, I pulled off at Albany and into the parking lot at Browsers' on my way home. Inside, the store was quiet but not empty—a young man lurked in the sci-fi section, not shopping, but deeply engrossed in a book he appeared to be reading. Abe was behind the counter, tinkering with online listings, responding to orders. When he saw me, he stood up. He was happy that I'd come to visit. I was happy to be there. I'd felt strange about bringing in the books I'd found at different thrift stores over the past few months: one of the forgotten novels that had been republished by the New York Review of Books, and a crisp new copy of Borges's *Labyrinths* with a glossy metallic cover. I didn't want anything for them, just to help them on their journey to a good home. Abe received them gladly.

We chatted about the different volumes of di Prima available online, whether they were worth the investment, or if they might be found in better condition. As we talked, I didn't feel hurried, like I needed to wrap it up, or even that I would need to buy something. Sometimes, when I visited Abe at his store, his wife would drop in—a kind, attractive woman who worked as a teacher. Abe's entire life was a place of welcome. I felt like a regular person who belonged exactly there, in that store, talking about books. I thought: *This is something I can do, want to do, want to be part of my life*. I can be part of the world of people who buy and sell books—not as a protagonist, a dealer—but as an interesting character you might find in a middle chapter. I could help advance the plot. And in this way, I could keep the connection to the world I'd grown up in, even if Michael wasn't around to connect me.

And then I did something weird. Buoyed by the enthusiasm Abe and I shared for the rarest of di Prima's works, and excited about what felt like a real connection with him, I asked Abe if he would help me find a first edition of *This Kind of Bird Flies Backward.* Surprising myself with this latent desire, I added a layer of complexity back into my relationship with Abe, but unlike me, he didn't blink. Abe would be glad to help find a copy, he said. They turn up from time to time.

With that, it only seemed right to leave, and so I drove home, ruminating again on the question of whether I'd jeopardized a friendship, or whether I might yet cure the ache I felt every time I thought about that book, and increasingly, every time I saw Michael.

❧

It occurred to me that, since I'd become a father, I was spending more time looking for used books. With two little boys, I certainly didn't have more time for this new hobby. And then I realized: hunting for books was how Michael parented me.

Even though he never made money, Michael is a good man. He was a good parent to me, teaching me his trade and sharing with me the obscure world he made for himself. Whatever Michael had, he gave to me without expectation of anything in return. Isn't that what it means to be a parent?

And then there was the wisdom he imparted to me as a book scout. Besides the vestiges of judgment I carry about authors, my apprenticeship with Michael helped me sketch out a trajectory to a life beyond the thrift stores and book sales around Eugene. The constant mental cataloging of titles, subjects, authors, categories of knowledge—all of it built a world that I could inhabit with almost any role, including my work in policy. Along with my mom, he'd helped prepare me for a career solid enough that I could be a person who takes care of others.

Abe hadn't grown up with book scouts. Though his family read, the fact remains that he grew up in Albany, bagging grass seed. The book world lured him in—for Abe, this was access to the broader world. To me, it seemed like a lifetime of struggle.

I had the instinct to mentor Abe, who was a generation behind me, even though he already knew more than I ever would about bookselling. What I wanted to tell him wasn't really about books. Maybe I wanted to tell him what I'd learned growing up with Michael: that bookselling was a fraught journey to an unhappy end. It's what I would tell my own boys when they asked about Michael.

But then, I thought, what pathway isn't a fraught journey to an unhappy ending? We know from stories that the struggle is the good part. As for the ending, time is undefeated. Whatever wisdom I might offer Abe, or eventually my own kids, it wouldn't mean more than Michael had taught me—to be myself, and to keep searching. Nothing will be easy, but if you keep going you can find your own rare first editions.

❧

Now, when the kids are busy with their activities, I contrive reasons to drive to Albany to hang around Browsers' with Abe. The pretext might be a book I'd seen the last time I was there, that I needed to go back for. A bibliography of Ezra Pound's early works published in periodicals, perhaps. When desperate, I'd gather a handful of books I'd found in thrift stores to bring to him, the pretext for my visit being that I wanted to help out by giving him yet another used copy of Borges's *Labyrinths* to sell.

Coming from work, I'd still be in my suit, maybe at least with the tie loosened. Often, he'd be engaged with a customer, chatting about a series of fantasy novels or letting some young truth-seeker know that yes, he does have a copy of the *Hitchhiker's Guide to the Galaxy*. When I was lucky, I'd find Abe alone at the register, puttering, available to receive me and my books and to chat about di Prima. We'd swap a quick round of *How are yous* and then, with no more need for niceties, our exchange would begin in earnest.

"Any news?" I asked.

"It's been a slow week. I check every day on several sites. Nothing new."

"Is it possible to, like, set an alert?"

"You can do that on some sites. But I worry that I would miss something."

"Makes sense," I said. I felt embarrassed for suggesting a workaround to a part of his job that he enjoyed. Like taking a caffeine pill instead of drinking coffee in the morning.

"I always think she should be more popular," Abe said. With this, we began the familiar routine of affirming our mutual love for di Prima. "She checks all the boxes. One of the Beats, but also kind of a revolutionary," Abe said. "She's, like, really cool."

"She is," I said. "That's why I think she's worth collecting. The interest will endure."

I used words like this—*endure*—because it made me feel like I was adding some kind of wisdom or perspective to the conversation. It would've been more sincere just to echo Abe's words. *Really cool.*

The bell on the door sounded and another customer came in behind me, and from the corner of my eye I saw a flash of camouflage moving quickly past the stacks and toward our confab at the register. While the intruder didn't ambush our conversation, I could feel his nervous energy behind me. It was familiar, the way he moved—the urgency to ask some burning question about a book he'd read, and to have his question received by Abe, who would understand why it mattered.

To allow an opportunity to the stranger behind me, I retreated to the poetry section to scan titles I'd seen a dozen times before. There, I found a trade edition of David Meltzer poems, underpriced at $4. When I made this kind of find in Abe's store—he knew who Meltzer was—I could never decide whether he'd planted the book for me or it was an oversight. I plucked the Meltzer for myself, thinking about what Abe was thinking about when he priced the book, and whether he was thinking about me.

Abe's poetry section was at the back of the store, and out of sight of the register, offering me the chance to observe his work with customers without being seen. Back at the register, the man in camo came at Abe with his questions locked and loaded.

"When I bought *Hunter* the other day, you seemed interested in it. Did you want to read it first before I bought it?"

The man in camo had literally bought a book called *Hunter*. He'd also been so charmed by Abe that he came back, as I had, in search of friendship. The difference, I hoped, was that Abe and I shared a love for di Prima, someone who nobody else in Albany has heard of. That's why Abe's reply surprised me.

"No worries," Abe said to the man in camo. "After you bought it, I actually ordered a copy for myself."

The hunter took time to respond. It was hard to believe, even for him, that Abe had bought another copy of the book.

"I didn't think—" the hunter started. "I guess you have some camo in you, huh. What I want to know," he continued, "is how did you know about pescatarians?"

This struck me as obvious because, in the Pacific Northwest, half of everyone says they're vegetarian, and within that half, half eat salmon anyway.

Earnestly, Abe explained how he'd come to know about fish-based diets. "I collect books about running, and they're always talking about what they eat. Some are fish-only, and one guy just eats fruit. Anyway, I always thought that was interesting. I eat everything."

"Ha!" said the hunter. "Me too. I just didn't know that other people knew about that. Okay. I have another one for you."

"Shoot," said Abe.

"I've been thinking about this word. But I can't remember what it means."

"Okay," said Abe. "What word is it?"

"Well," said the hunter. "The word I'm thinking about is *convergence*. But I'm not sure it's the right word. I think it's about when computers start to take over."

"I think I know what word it is," said Abe. "They used to say 'convergence' sometimes. Now I think they mostly say 'singularity,' like when AI takes over."

"That's the word! I knew you would know it," said Camo. "One last question for you."

"Okay," said Abe. "These are good questions."

"I thought so," said Camo. "Okay, here it is. Can you use paper bags, like to give to people when they buy books?"

Abe took his time to answer. From the poetry section, I could hear the gears grinding in Abe's head: *This man wants to bring me his used grocery bags, and my choices are to reject the offer, or to do his recycling for him.*

"I can always use bags," Abe said.

"That's great! I'm the kind of guy who never likes to throw anything away. I'll come by tomorrow."

With that, Camo left with the same urgency he'd brought in, his spirits lifted by having tracked down 'singularity' but also, I could imagine, by finding a purpose for his bags. What does anyone really want except to be useful? Or maybe just understood.

CHAPTER 14

Crooked House

After the measured success of our trip to Passages to liberate some modest volumes of the *Floating Bear*, both Abe and Gerry craved the comfort of a store whose books and ambience more closely aligned with their own instincts. At Gerry's suggestion, we piled back into my Prius and headed for Crooked House Books & Paper up in Portland's Broadway district.

Crooked House had been around for twenty years, but it had been only two years since Scott Givens took over. He'd sold Browsers' to Abe and left behind his life in sleepy Albany for the weirdness of Portland and the Broadway neighborhood. Like Browsers', Crooked House occupied a residential house, an old craftsman home on a narrow lane near the vortex where Broadway and Sandy Boulevards are bisected by the interstate. If you want to find a good cup of coffee and complain about how much Portland has changed, you're better off in the Alberta or Hawthorne neighborhoods.

If you happened to find your way to Crooked House, it was almost certainly because you'd planned to visit, as we had, and not because you chanced upon it. Which is why, when I parked the Prius in front of the bookstore, I was surprised to see a sign that said "Open, by chance." As we walked up the steps into the store, Gerry explained that Scott would tend to his retail operation depending on his mood, and that today, we were lucky. Abe opened Browsers' unfailingly from 10 a.m. to 6 p.m. His mood never faltered. Having heard about Scott's mercurial humor from Abe and Gerry, I was nervous to meet him.

It was odd, in middle age, to feel the teenage excitement of going to a party. Ahead of me, Abe and Gerry spilled into the store, where Scott was sitting at a computer, pensive in his beanie and on-trend glasses, as Portland as rain and beer. His new aesthetic would have been out of place in Albany. Scott looked like he'd been through enough, in his work and his life, that he was not going to be troubled by whatever silliness came through the door of his store. He looked like he might be in his early fifties, maybe a decade ahead of me and a couple decades behind Michael and Gerry. In his sheer middle-agedness, Scott reminded me of myself—unexcitable, expecting disaster. His disinterest in interacting with others seemed to be conditioned by something darker, some kind of experience that my own life had not yet wrought on me.

After greeting Scott, we fanned out across the store, looking for alphabetized shelves to give order to our thoughts. I couldn't find poetry at first glance, so I resorted to fiction despite my misgivings, passed down from Michael, about ever spending money on it. There, I found a curated collection of literature unlike any I'd ever seen before. I didn't see any of the books I knew to search for, from Carver to Kittredge to Vonnegut. Instead, the fiction section consisted of novels published before 1970, each with some memorable title or decorous cover. There were westerns and romance books and books in translation by writers long forgotten by American readers. The stock must have been selected, curated really, for the curiosity it provoked. I struggled to map this bookstore onto everything I'd known about the business.

After an initial pass around the store, Abe and Gerry gathered around Scott, who had been boss to both of them for long chapters of their lives.

"Where did you get this?" Gerry asked, holding a hardback volume of *Gabriela* by Jorge Amado, the Brazilian writer, with a lovely watercolor on its cover. It was the kind of book I'd skip over at the thrift store, knowing that despite its intrigue, nobody would ever actually read it. Except, I saw now, that Gerry might, and that this was the kind of store with books that would interest him.

"It was part of a buy I made a couple months ago," Scott said. He hardly looked up from his computer, even as Gerry talked to him.

"Hey, did you go down to the LA Rare Book Fair this year?" Gerry asked.

"Yeah," Scott said. "I'm still unpacking from it."

I knew how badly Gerry wanted to talk about LA and the fair. Scott was closed off, even from Gerry.

With Abe it was different. Abe knelt at the stacks of books closest to Scott's desk, like a dog at its owner's feet, as he scanned for first editions and signatures.

"How do you feel about CDs?" Scott asked.

"You mean like compact discs?" It was a natural question from a twenty-five-year-old.

"Yeah," said Scott. "I bought a collection of them. Would you want to list them?"

"I could do that," said Abe.

Even from across the store, where I lurked in the fiction section, I could see that this transaction was something tender, almost intimate. Abe had bought Browsers' from Scott on terms so friendly that it was hardly business at all, more like an inheritance. The opportunity that Scott was offering to Abe now, to sell CDs, might be beneficial in some small way to Scott's finances, but was more likely to be an additional source of income that Abe could draw on at Browsers'. The blend of generosity and self-preservation had echoes of parenting.

Gerry butted in, holding an oversized collector's edition of Stephen Crane's *The Red Badge of Courage*. As required reading still at some high schools, and past its seventy-five years of copyright protection, the book was the kind of thing that nobody would ever spend money on. "Abe," Gerry said. "You should take this down to Browsers' and get one of your customers to buy it."

I thought Gerry was joking, but Abe received the book from him and added it to a pile he'd gathered from among Scott's stacks. Like Browsers', back when Scott still owned it, Crooked House had piles of books everywhere, from the floor teetering up to your waist. Abe was expertly picking from these piles without knocking them over, collecting odd volumes to take back to Albany. *The Red Badge of Courage*, I thought initially, was Gerry ribbing Abe for the less discerning customers that Browsers' served in Albany. But when Abe added it to his stack, it became more nourishment to be passed from Scott to Abe, for Abe to receive and use to sustain himself.

As Abe and Scott did business, and Gerry bantered with them both, I longed to join the conversation. I took tentative steps toward them but there was no reasonable pretext for my involvement in their world. When I thought about complimenting the store, my own mental drafts about the uniqueness of Scott's books made me cringe. Despite the fondness between the bookmen, this wasn't a place for platitudes. Even to compare Crooked House to Browsers' would touch too directly on the genuine connection between all of them.

Forced to remain in the fiction section, I found a book of Wallace Stegner's musings about the American novel, published in Japan in 1952, when Stegner served as a writer in residence at a Tokyo university. It was a paperback and not particularly cheap at $25, but I'd never seen it in my years of scanning shelves for Stegner. As I flipped through it, I realized that I also wanted to read it. Finally, with no pretextual comment ready, I drifted toward Scott's desk and lingered as the others talked shop. I scanned the books that Scott kept behind his desk, acting as casual as I could. Keeping my eyes down, I noticed that Scott wasn't wearing shoes. This surprised me; going shoeless was not something I'd ever seen Michael or any other bookstore owner do. Instead of shoes, Scott wore a pair of bright-pink socks, almost like they'd been chosen to pierce through the muted colors of his middle-aged Portlander garb. His empty

Birkenstocks sat next to the desk. For someone so terse, Scott also seemed at ease with himself.

"Are you looking for anything in particular?" he asked.

As I looked up, I wasn't sure if Scott had asked because I was staring at his feet. I processed the question, waiting for words to form. "Do you have anything by William Stafford?"

Stafford was Oregon's first poet laureate. Any bookstore in Oregon would have something by him, I figured, so it would give me a chance to open up a conversation with Scott without yet revealing my deeper interest in di Prima. I wanted to keep my powder dry.

Scott stood and directed me to the poetry section. I had caught his attention, I thought, and I might yet be able to talk to him. If I could think of another entry, I might get him to tell me about his own interest in books and bookstores. The poetry section was only about five steps from his desk, tucked into a nook at the back of the store, leaving me precious little time to think of my next subject. Then, Scott said, "There's a first edition of Stafford's first book. Maybe you have it."

He'd called my bluff. The only Stafford I owned was *The Way It Is*, a trade paperback edition of collected works, the kind of thing published for readers, not collectors. I had no idea what Stafford's first book was, when it was published, or how much it might be worth, signed or unsigned. I knew virtually nothing about the books of the author I'd asked about.

"Yes," I answered. What I meant was, *Yes, I have this book, and if even I don't, then yes, I'm willing to lie so that you might think I know what I'm talking about.* Since I'd answered with one word, curtly, and made no gesture toward the volumes of Stafford on the shelf, Scott had no choice but to leave me staring blankly at the book I said I had.

At least I had escaped fiction and was now on more familiar footing, in the poetry section. Plus, I was tucked into the back of the store, out of view from Scott and Abe and Gerry and left to collect my thoughts. Ignoring Stafford, I sorted through some early volumes by Snyder, including an early edition of *Riprap and Cold Mountain Poems* published as part of the Four Seasons Writing series. I plucked it confidently from the shelf, gathered my wits, and returned to the conversation around Scott's desk.

Gerry, I noticed, had amassed a tall stack of books by forgotten authors and, after a discount, wrote out a check for several hundred dollars to Scott. I was no longer accustomed to seeing checkbooks in action, but if anyone was good for it, it was Gerry.

Abe approached with his own stack. Scott eyeballed it and said, "Figure out what you think they're worth and then you can pay me something when you sell them."

I paid last for my Snyder and my Stegner. After what had happened with David at Passages, I was surprised to receive a discount. Scott examined the Stegner as he slipped it into a bag. "Good scouting," he said.

Whether the book was worth a penny more than its $25 price, and even if it was mere flattery of a customer, I liked the compliment. I wanted Scott to see me as a person who knew something about books, as a person worth knowing.

We book scouts were hungry after our hard work. Gerry suggested lunch. Abe used his phone to look for places, but nearby restaurants predictably had what Abe considered to be Portland prices.

"You guys like burgers?" Scott asked.

"I'll eat anything," Abe said. "I'm always hungry."

"I'll eat anything if it's cheap," Gerry said. I recalled him spending hundreds of dollars on books each time I'd see him. "You hungry, Scott?"

"No. But I'll drink a beer." He slipped his pink socks into his Birkenstocks, and we made the trip to the smash-burger joint on Sandy, five blocks up from Crooked House. It was a charmless setting, some years after the smash-burger craze first swept through, and the service was perfectly indifferent. Gerry paid for all of us.

"The genuine Portland experience," Scott said, sipping his beer.

We talked shop while our burgers were getting smashed. Scott and Abe checked in about regulars at Browsers', the ones who had frequented the store when Scott was there and who continued on after Abe took over. One customer who visited the store from Eugene, where he worked as a metalsmith, had purchased an early first edition of a science fiction novel on an installment plan, for thousands of dollars. He had the kind of income that didn't come in steady streams, but he was a regular visitor at the store. The irrationality of Scott's decision to sell the book on credit to such a customer tugged at my bureaucratic incredulity.

"You gave thousands of dollars of credit to a metalsmith from Eugene?" I asked. The question itself struck me as funny, in line with their banter. It was my first reentry into the collective conversation since falling flat on my inquiry about William Stafford.

"He's a good person," Scott said. "He reached out when I lost someone unexpectedly. He understood what I was going through."

Swallowing my regret for having doubted Scott, I wanted to know more about the connection he'd made with the metalsmith—how they'd bonded over something besides books. Whom had Scott lost? What had the metalsmith understood? I felt jealous that the metalsmith had proven capable of bringing comfort to another person after a loss. I hadn't done this yet in my life. I didn't know if I could.

The conversation veered to a topic that delighted the bookmen: theft. As with any valuable, thieves were attracted to books, but because of the specialized knowledge required to identify their value, the thief didn't always know what to take. I recalled Michael laughing about someone stealing an old magazine with Janis Joplin on the cover from one of his many stores. Gerry had told me about one of David Abel's earlier stores where the cost to repair the window smashed by the thief was more than the value of the stolen books. Plus, as David recounted to interested parties, Patti Smith had sent him a letter of condolence. One of her books was among those stolen.

Scott told us about a robbery that was big enough to get coverage in Portland's newspaper. A collector of comic books, along with signed first editions by horror writers such as Stephen King, had passed away in his home. Stephen King rarely signed books, and his earliest first editions are zealously sought by devotees, so this collection was of interest. The *Oregonian* published an obituary about the dead collector and described the collection, which alerted would-be thieves to the presence of the valuables that remained in the unoccupied home. "It was like putting up a sign on the house to say, 'Come steal all these expensive books,'" Scott said.

The thief had been mainly interested in the comic books, and according to Scott's sources, had been able to unload many of them to unscrupulous buyers. When it came to used books, though, the prospective buyers in town mostly belonged to the Cascade Booksellers Association, which had alerted its members about the stolen books. A bookseller who buys books that are later discovered to be stolen typically loses his or her investment. This possibility makes any purchase of a large collection unnerving, unless the buyer can be sure of the books' provenance.

"Even though everyone knew these signed Stephen Kings were out there, and they were stolen, I still wanted to see them," Scott said. "They're worth a fortune. So when this guy comes into Crooked House and says, 'I have some Stephen Kings and they're signed,' my first thought was, 'I'm going to buy them just to have my hands on them,'" he said. "Of course, everyone knows they're stolen, so you're not going to do that. Only the comic-book guys can get away with it. I called the police and they arrested the guy."

Scott had a desire to possess something he knew he couldn't keep. At that table, we all knew how he felt. We finished our burgers, thinking about what it might be like to get our hands on a collection of signed first editions of Stephen King, a crown jewel for a collector no matter how little you care about Stephen King.

"Do you guys want to come to the warehouse?" Scott asked.

Gerry and Abe both nodded.

I didn't know where we were headed. We piled into my Prius and took a ramp over I-84 and then down onto a sliver of land tucked next to the freeway. The ramp had only one destination: a storage building occupying an unlikely pocket between the freeway and the light-rail tracks. It felt like the kind of place you needed special permission to visit.

The storage buildings were large and imposing and no one else was around. We parked the Prius, and Scott found a dolly to bring into his unit at the center of the labyrinthine building. There, he lifted the door to his unit, revealing hundreds of boxes full of books, stacked in columns as high as our heads.

Gerry and Abe said nothing and began to work their way into the stacks, opening boxes and rifling through them. Scott said he'd bought some of the books from a collector, some from another estate. One other dealer had visited the warehouse, but most of the boxes were untouched. Inside the boxes were thousands of books, whole collections that had belonged to people who'd built them lovingly before leaving the earth. Now the books lived in a spooky building next to the freeway.

I opened a box and found books about theater and photography. I had no idea what they were worth, or what I was supposed to do next. I set them back in the boxes, doing my best not to disturb the precise way in which they were packed. Gerry, on the other side of the storage unit, emptied his boxes out fully, inspecting individual books and making a pile of those he planned to keep. Abe worked on his knees like a plumber inspecting pipes. Scott looked out over his inventory. He was quiet, thinking.

Reluctant to disturb the contents of another box, I drifted toward Gerry. He showed me several of his finds—again, mostly literature in translation, mostly worthless. But he was high with excitement at the prospect of the nearly virgin collection.

"This is the dark side of the business," Gerry said. He handed a small red hardback to me. "Here," he said. "This is a good one for you."

I inspected the book. It was published in the nineteenth century, about the literary history of London in the century before. Gerry was giving me the same gentle ribbing he'd given to Abe: handing me a worthless book and telling me to find a home for it. It was a joke, but also, I sensed, a gesture of friendship.

Both Scott and Gerry handed books to Abe to sell at Browsers'—books that were uninteresting to their cultured way of thinking, and therefore, more appropriate for Albany. Abe received these books in the friendly spirit in which they were offered, while also quietly collecting a handful of interesting books about jazz and a spare volume or two of poetry.

As thrilled as I was to see this side of the business, I did not have the instinct that came naturally to Abe and Gerry to sort through the boxes of books. Instead, I pawed at Gerry's rejects and inspected Abe's keepers. Next time I'm in Browsers', I figured, I could buy from among the books that Abe plucked, such as the book about jazz by the poet Philip Larkin.

Along with the literary history of London assigned to me, I found a copy of *Rotten Ralph*, which I remembered from my childhood. Ralph was a monkey who did all kinds of terrible things. I was not a perfect child, and I wondered now if Michael had been trying to tell me something when he first gave the book to me. More likely, he'd found it cheap and didn't think much more about it. I wondered whether my own kids should read it.

When we were done, or at least Abe and Gerry had satisfied their desire to dig through boxes, a series of intricate transactions began. Scott suggested that Abe and Gerry, once they returned home and had a chance to inspect the books, determine a fair price to pay for them. This arrangement was built on years of understanding, knowing that Gerry had a strong sense of value, and that Abe would quickly look his books up online. It was also about trust: Scott knew that these were honest bookmen who would pay him fairly. When Scott extended the same courtesy to me, I wasn't sure how I would begin to assess the value of my books, either the literary history or *Rotten Ralph*.

"I don't know how to do that," I told Scott. "I'm not like them."

Scott nodded. He flipped through the *Rotten Ralph*. "This is a great book," he said.

"I know," I said.

"Ten dollars for them both," he said.

I found a bill in my wallet.

On the drive back from Portland, I was relieved that nobody wanted to talk about books or bookstores. In the backseat of the Prius, Abe was quiet, withdrawn after a day of complex transactions.

Gerry, even after the trip to what he had called the dark side, was his same affable self. He talked to me about baseball, about the Dodgers and Giants and about free agents who had gone unsigned that off-season, young men who had lost their place in the league. Gerry had recalled how, as a kid hanging around Michael's stores, I'd been interested in just about everything else out there in the world besides books. After our day together, this desire to think about something else had returned, and I was grateful to Gerry for the generosity of his conversation.

CHAPTER 15

Mother Foucault's

I'd seen the dark side, and I wanted more. It wasn't because of the books, either—*Rotten Ralph* was a reading copy, and the literary history of London that Gerry stuck me with was worth even less. It was the kind of book, old and cloyingly literary, that might impress an amateur. I thought about giving it to my partner.

It was Scott who was on my mind. His story, or what I'd inferred about his story, had formed a sort of mystery that intrigued me. Against all odds, Scott had created a thriving bookstore in Albany, Oregon, a place known for its lingering smell and rare metals, but never for its intellectual life. After his bookstore had become a successful business and an essential part of the community, Scott gave it up, and seemingly for so little, so that Abe could take a chance at living this life. This was not the kind of gesture I'd ever known another bookseller to make. Even Michael, tired of trips to the post office to sell his online inventory, had never offered to pass his books to me. What was a bookseller without his collection?

Abe and Gerry had hinted that the decision to leave Browsers' and Albany had to do with Scott's personal life, but it didn't explain how he'd ended up wearing pink socks, ferrying books to and from the dark side. It was as if, in letting go of Browsers' and transitioning to Crooked House, he'd transformed along the way.

I found an article in the local paper published when Scott left Browsers', noting how the store had become an institution for local readers. The Albany *Democrat-Herald* had seen the same angle that had intrigued me: that Albany, of all places, had produced an exceptional bookstore, and it had endured.

Then, further down, I found the website for Crooked House Books & Paper and clicked through. What revealed itself on the website was the distinct vision that I'd seen when we visited Scott—a collection of books carefully curated around an aesthetic—but the vision was even more precise online. Crooked House, I thought, could not have come from the same mind behind Browsers'. If visiting a used bookstore was like looking around inside someone's head, except for the clutter at both Browsers' and Crooked House, the stores had stemmed from different kinds of thinkers.

As I searched online for details about Crooked House, I found a link to a page on the Crooked House website for the Rachelle Markley Memorial Fund. There, I read:

> The founder of Crooked House Books & Paper passed away unexpectedly on August 26, 2022.
>
> Rachelle Markley was born November 19, 1962, in Piqua, Ohio. She was raised in Phoenix and graduated from Phoenix College. She worked in mental health care for several years, then managed a bakery where she explored her love of cooking. In 2003, she moved to Portland and started working in the book industry. Over the next twenty years, she worked in new books, she owned a small used bookstore, and she eventually opened Crooked House Books & Paper, an antiquarian shop which specialized in books by, for, and about women. She was the organizer of the Rose City Book and Paper Fair and one of the key members of Cascade Booksellers Association, serving as its first president.

❧

I had not expected Scott's story to reveal itself so openly, so publicly. It made my heart ache. I'll never know the details of what happened, but the nuts and bolts of the story, confirmed by Scott and Gerry, are that Scott left his store and his life in Albany to be in Portland with Rachelle, working together to run Crooked House and the Cascade Booksellers Association. Rachelle, to those who knew her, was lively and full of the same rich sense of humor that Scott had, only she had more of it and was quicker to share it. Scott, you might infer, had found something rare: a woman in the used book trade, sure enough of herself and her place in the business that she came to be a leader in it, with a unique vision for a store and the chops to do good business across decades. She was a partner for Scott in his way of being in the world, another bird who flies backward.

In their short time together, Scott and Rachelle published a book of cocktail recipes, with citations and images from books they'd each unearthed along their journeys. They published a catalog of cookbooks, and given the unique stock at Crooked House, likely had plans for more.

In the eerie solitude of an open browser, I took one more step toward the abyss and searched just for Rachelle Markley. I guess I wanted to see what I could learn about the partner Scott had lost. She had made a light impression on the digital world, with a few results related to Crooked House and a handful of poems she had published back in 2001 as a student. I found a single photo of Rachelle taken next to her collection at a book fair. She had short bangs and hipster glasses and a warm, sincere smile full of mischief and mirth. Like the mystery surrounding Scott, this brief hint of Rachelle's life made you want to know more about her.

Based on the timeline of when he left Browsers' to Abe, Scott couldn't have been with Rachelle for more than a year or two before she passed. He had mentioned, in the context of the metalsmith, that his loss was unexpected. Now he occupied the house of Crooked House alone—shoes off, opening the store when grief allowed.

I wanted to talk to Scott, to hear the story in his words. I wasn't sure why I thought so, but I figured he might know something that would be helpful to me eventually. The gnawing feeling in my own belly that I associated with di Prima, I sensed, was really about Michael. Scott knew something I hadn't learned about yet—not the feeling of a fantasy slipping through your fingers, but the pang of loss, plain and simple. One day Michael wouldn't be there, and I would be alone with the story of what happened to our copy of *This Kind.*

❧

To take a day off work for a mid-level state employee is no small investment. I get exactly twelve days of paid leave each year. When I took my job, I tried to negotiate for more, but I was told that paid leave accumulates at the same rate for all employees in my classification and unit. This was the first of many small discomforts that would eventually become my nourishment, my daily bread, as a servant of the state.

When I exchanged emails with Scott and asked if we could talk more at his store, he replied, *I could plan to be there*, and I submitted the request to use a precious day off. It was worth it, I thought, for this chance at friendship in the throes of middle age. I'd connected with Abe and Gerry, sure, but Scott was the brains behind Browsers', he knew something about loss, and I believed that we might see the world in a similar way.

I drove up to Portland distractedly, thinking about what I hoped to learn from Scott. I wanted to hear about Crooked House and Rachelle, but there was no way I could come out directly and ask him about something so personal, so painful. I would have to be economical with any questions, to let him say as much as he wanted to, not more. I'd ask him where he came from originally, and how he got into the book business. Then I'd ask about Browsers'. He'd want to talk about his old store, I figured, if he was anything like Michael. Then I'd ask him about Abe and Gerry, our mutual acquaintances. Once Scott knew I was part of this world, it'd be safe to ask him how he came to Crooked House, and about what he'd lost along the way.

Arriving in Portland, I parked across the street from the store, pausing to take it in from the window of my car. Like most of the two-story craftsman homes in Northeast Portland built in the early twentieth century, it had a severe roof pinching a couple of bedrooms above a tightly packed main floor—living room, dining room, and kitchen. The whole of the house leaned forward and slightly to the left as you faced it. The artful but half-neglected flowers and plants framing the old house added to the messy charm.

Nervous, I left the car and climbed the steps up to the porch of the old house, where I noticed the various webs and desiccated moths that had accumulated around the porch light. I gave a firm knock on the door and waited on the porch, watching the street as rain came down slowly at first, and then in torrents. It was the kind of rain that soaks you for the rest of the day. I peeked inside the window and saw only a dim light from the back of the house, the kind you leave on to make passersby think someone is home when you're away.

Planted in front of the crooked old house is a hand-painted sign for the bookstore. Dangling below it is another small sign, about the size of an envelope, that says: *Until we meet again, linger in your own company.* You wouldn't notice this sign unless you were trying, like I was, to hear what the store was telling me. It struck me that the sign was left by Rachelle, who gave Crooked House to Scott when she passed. She may have intended these words for him and for other visitors to the store, and now, having come to see the small sign from this angle, it would become my directive also.

I didn't bother to knock again because I knew Scott wasn't there. I let go and walked down into the rain.

❧

In my own company, I set off to wander around the Hollywood District. After the clouds had finished their labor, the sun cut through, slicing down to the wet streets, producing a glare and the gravelly smell of steam rising from the asphalt. Windshield wipers screeched on cars passing by—the ones whose drivers hadn't noticed that the rain had stopped. Homeless folks who had framed themselves in doorways began to re-emerge.

In the sunlight, I started to shake myself loose from the web of story and feeling that had drawn me to Scott. Across Sandy Boulevard, I ducked into the old Hollywood Antique Mall, with its checkered floors and a gallery of struggling businesses. Downstairs was an inestimable number of square feet of antique furniture and bric-a-brac that I wanted no part of. These were the worst places to try to find books—from dealers obsessed about car repair manuals and old books about dolls. But something about the small businesses in the gallery—the Tibetan candy shop, the African hair salon—drew me further in.

At the back of the mall, I found a café earnestly committed to no-frills sandwiches. It had no sourced ingredients or artisan touches, just sliced bread with piles of meat and cheese and basic condiments. No other customers were present. Somewhere else, this might've deterred me, but at this juncture, I needed the sandwich.

At the counter, I heard Michael's voice speaking through me.

"Smoked turkey," I said. "Dark rye."

"You got it. Cheese?"

"Swiss. And lettuce and tomato."

"You want mayo on that?"

"Just mustard," I said.

"You got it."

My sandwich came to the table in a plastic basket with no napkin. It was dripping with mustard. As I ate, I wiped my mouth with one sleeve of my jacket and then the other, and when I was finished, I rubbed my sleeves together to massage the mustard in so that it wouldn't be so obvious. It left a yellow sheen on the sleeves of my jacket, still visible but only if you were looking for it.

I didn't know why Scott had skipped our meeting, but I could imagine. In his shoes, I'd have done the same. Why was some random state employee so interested in making special plans to visit the store?

It didn't matter. I had a day off work and a good lunch in my stomach. I asked myself what Michael would do with a full belly and a free afternoon, and the answer was obvious enough: look for books.

I headed over to a bookstore called Mother Foucault's, which was close to the freeway in Southeast Portland and on the way home for me anyway. I'd heard Abe and Gerry talk about this store like it was something strange, even for them. Given the store's name and the way Gerry had talked it up, I figured it would be another David Abel situation. But what I found there, I could not have expected.

Mother Foucault's was in an old building in Portland's inner east side, in the ribbon of city between warehouses and homeless services. Traffic from the freeway and bridges overwhelmed my senses. Homeless folks stirred gently in the folds of this landscape and the gray of its sounds.

Entering the bookstore, I was welcomed by an old kitchen table topped with neat stacks of books, arranged but not in any order that I could discern. The stacks reminded me of tidepools where ideas washed up in patterns that were both predictable and unique. To the right of this table was a counter with similar stacks except higher, and behind the counter, an aging man who appeared to be reading a philosophy tract in the original German. Walter Benjamin unpacking his library.

Deeper in, without signage, fiction unfolded across the store, much of it published in languages other than English. This included novels in their original language, novels translated from English to other languages, and novels written in a language other than English and translated to a different language, other than English. It was a collection that Gerry Rouff, and perhaps the odd graduate student, would love. I marveled at shelves stocked with lesser-known voices of the Latin American boom—Julio Cortazar, Mario Benedetti—next to obscure masterpieces of French, Italian, and Spanish literature and the rare American writer—Faulkner, mainly—who ascended to their orbit.

Given the mixed success of my day so far, I was desperate to buy a book for myself, even if it was only something to read. I found a novel by Elena Ferrante, recommended by the *New Yorker*, but it turned out to be translated into Spanish from the original Italian. Mercifully, as I worked back toward the beginning of the alphabet, I plucked a bibliography listing all of William S. Burroughs's works published between 1955 and 1973. I did not intend to collect Burroughs or even to read him again if I could avoid it. Bibliographies could make for good reading in their own way, mapping the journey of an author's ideas as they made their way out into the world. Priced at $12, the book was a bargain even without a dust jacket.

Checking the price of the Burroughs and other books, I saw that they were not indexed for online sale. Usually a book has, in pencil, a number from the store's database, either next to the price or tucked in near the spine. Without this notation, it appeared that Mother Foucault's was not listing its books. It was also possible that the store was not checking other online listings when pricing its books. It was as though Mother Foucault's operated with the conviction that each book had its own innate value, not to be diminished by the banality of supply and demand. Most books I inspected were priced at exactly $12—except for an occasional volume listed for $100, for reasons that were not obvious to me.

As I crossed through the labyrinth to pay the old philosopher, one more book caught my eye: *Silverview*, the final work by the great spy novelist John le Carré. I couldn't figure what it was doing here, planted, like a drop point, among old ethics tracts and nineteenth-century French novels. I could read it on my next vacation. I brought the le Carré and the Burroughs to the desk, where the philosopher marshaled us through our transaction with as few words as possible.

I left Mother Foucault's feeling no less lost, no less lonely than I had outside of Crooked House. On a workday, in a city that feels both large and small, both strange and familiar, I couldn't shake the feeling that I was somewhere I wasn't supposed to be. Again, I thought of Michael and how to spend the rest of an idle afternoon. I could visit Powell's, and maybe just being there, seeing it again, would feel comforting. On the other hand, it seemed like a good idea to get out of Portland.

I climbed back into the Prius and followed my instincts, which led me south on I-5, past Salem, and back down to Albany. Browsers' wouldn't be open—it being Monday—but Albany was the antidote to Portland. Its downtown rhymed cheerfully with the Hollywood District— built around the same time, but with less gloom around its renovated movie theater and its farmers' market. Albany didn't struggle the way Portland did.

It also had a thrift store with books that never got picked over. Helping Hands sells donated wares to fund a homeless shelter that's often in the news for one scandal or another. In a cold and grimy warehouse on First Avenue in Albany, it would be impossible to imagine Scott or even Abe visiting the store to scout. This made it a good place to search for books.

The shelves were full of the same books that had been there for years—Bob Woodward exposés and a half-dozen copies of Kitty Kelly's biography of Ronald Reagan. For fiction, there was no shortage of romance novels and dog-eared mysteries to go with an underlined copy of Robinson Crusoe. But there, in the half shelf devoted to literature, was an interesting title: *Baudelaire and Freud*, by Leo Bersani.

You had to be careful with books of secondary scholarship on Freud. There was no shortage of intellectual lightweights riding his coattails. Baudelaire, however, is another story. There would always be a market, always enough curiosity, to pick up the old Parisian. More interesting than that, Leo Bersani himself had become known later in his career for his scholarship on the AIDS epidemic. In short, there were too many books about Freud, not enough about Baudelaire, and eventually there would be more about Bersani.

As I leafed through folios in the poetry section, a small boy wandered over—maybe seven or eight, about the size of my oldest. I don't know why he was in the aisle with poetry, drama, and literary criticism, but I pictured his adult in another part of the store, scanning shelves for resalable stock. Maybe it was vinyl records or vintage clothing—the Pendleton shirts that people sold now on eBay.

Whatever the boy was doing there at Helping Hands, it wasn't his first time. He knew all the words to the classic rock song on the radio, the kind that sounds innocuous until you listen carefully to the words. "Sometimes, love don't feel like it should. You make it hurt so good."

I needed to leave, without even checking fiction. It was worthless anyway. More than that, I needed to get away from myself and from the small boy who would one day have his own books to search for. I paid fifty cents for the Bersani and escaped back to the Prius, where I closed my eyes and traced backward through the confluence of people and events that had brought me to the Helping Hands thrift store in Albany.

It was late afternoon now and there was just enough sun breaking through the clouds that I felt a kind of hazy churn in my stomach, not quite nausea, not quite hunger. Whatever it was, I was far from satisfied, having burnt the vacation day to buy a handful of odd books. I could scout the Book Bin in Corvallis, but even in desperation I couldn't force myself any further.

"Fuck it," I said, finally, and headed to BJ's Ice Cream on the old Highway 20 in Albany.

There, I read a sign on the wall that the ice cream's fat content is 14.6 percent. I had no idea if this was a little bit of milk fat or a lot, but it seemed significant. No one else was in the shop, just myself and the person serving ice cream, so I felt no obligation to order something respectable, like mint chocolate chip or even salted caramel. Instead, I let my desire loose and ordered a sugar cone with a tall scoop of cotton candy ice cream.

On the drive back down to Eugene, the ice cream melted and ran down the cone onto my leg. With mustard already smeared into my sleeves, I stopped caring and let it fall, leaving bright pink splotches on my pants. I went instinctively to Michael's house instead of my own. There, I spotted him standing out in his driveway, staring blankly across the street at the Dari Mart. He may have been in between chores—it was hard to tell anymore. Mostly, it felt like he was waiting for me. When I parked and got out of the car, he resumed a conversation from days ago, in midstream. He thought constantly about his books, and at least that afternoon, he was also thinking about me.

"You want the collection of John Berryman poems? It's too banged up to list. I could probably get $15 for it, but why bother."

He was making a gift. There was no occasion, and he made sure you understood that he didn't value what he gave. But it was a gift nonetheless, and after the day I'd had, I was grateful.

"I don't even like Berryman," I said, which is true. He was a complicated, unhappy writer. "But I'll take it." I reached into my back seat and pulled out Bersani's book on Baudelaire and Freud. "Here," I said. "You can sell this Bersani."

"Who's Bersani?" Michael said.

"You never heard of Leo Bersani?"

"Oh, you mean Leo Bersani, the guy who wrote the book," Michael said.

"Yeah, that's the guy," I said. "Everyone's into Bersani right now."

"He's a helluva guy, Bersani," Michael said.

And with our business concluded, I got back into the Prius, drove home, and called it a day.

CHAPTER 16

Partial Eclipse

The eclipse over Eugene that spring was only partial, not like the totality that moved from Texas through the mid-Atlantic states. Still, talk of the eclipse was in the news and online and I wanted to see it, if only to say that I did. After my morning work meetings, I stepped outside with no firm plans, just the hope of seeing something to remind me of my relative place in the scheme of things.

I walked over to the outdoor store, which sold specialized viewing glasses for the eclipse but only in packs of four. I bought a pack and kept on walking, all the way to the Whiteaker neighborhood to see whether Michael and my mom were home—they were always home—and to watch the partial eclipse with them. When I got to the front porch, I could hear public radio blasting in the living room, thoughtful voices describing the momentary darkness over Mississippi. I pounded on the door. After a minute, I pounded again. Michael answered, looking like he'd just woken up.

Without greeting me, he turned around and yelled, "It's Danny. Danny's here."

From the back of the house, "What?" My mom, evidently, was still in bed.

"Danny's here," Michael repeated. "You better come see him."

They know I go by Daniel at work and in my own home. It doesn't matter.

My mom ambled forward from the back of the house, blinking. "Oh, Danny's here! Why didn't you tell me?"

"I told you, Danny's here."

"I'm here," I added.

"What are you doing here?" Michael asked.

I pointed at the radio, still blaring. "The eclipse," I shouted. "It's happening." I held up the package with four sets of glasses.

"But we don't have glasses," my mom said.

"I brought glasses," I said, waving them in front of her.

"Danny brought glasses," she said to Michael.

"To see the eclipse?" Michael asked, turning down the radio.

"Yes," I said, softening my voice, having vanquished NPR.

"What?" my mom asked.

"These are eclipse glasses," I said.

"Danny brought eclipse glasses," my mom said to Michael, again.

"Why aren't we watching the eclipse?" Michael asked.

I followed them out to the porch and down the three short steps that they both now struggled with, even with a recently installed handrail.

The three of us scanned the sky with our dark glasses. I was the first to find the sun, which looked so much smaller than the light and heat that came off of it. I noticed the chunk bitten off by the moon, like a cookie that's been nibbled. A partial eclipse.

I took off my glasses and looked over at Michael and my mom, each of their heads rolling on their necks, their eyes peering through the glasses, searching for the sun. The clouds that had been moving through all morning had thickened and, just now, had inched across to cover the view of the moon blocking a small part of the sun.

"It's too cloudy," I said.

"It's always too damn cloudy," Michael said.

"It's okay," my mom said. "I'm just glad whenever you come over." She retreated from the porch back into the house to resume work on one of her projects.

"Want to see some books?" Michael asked. I wanted to leave, to get back to work and the predictable rhythms of my desk, but I couldn't think of any reason why I needed to. Michael always wanted to show me his books. He'd get me to look at them one way or another. It was easier to give in.

In his small office, Michael held out a stack of trade paperbacks on various subjects that he'd bought from some kind of junk seller down in Cottage Grove, about a half-hour south of Eugene. He'd been turned on to this seller by a friend, Ollie, who was always involved in sales and transactions of various kinds. Michael was excited because he'd paid only a dollar each for the books, and the thrift stores and library sales almost always charge two. A few of the books, he thought, would sell online for twenty. They were interesting books but hardly the kind of thing you would imagine someone going out of their way to buy. A collection of the letters of Thomas Wolfe, a novelist from the early twentieth century. The complete short stories of Bernard Malamud. It was the kind of stock you might be able to trade in somewhere. Michael had spent an hour driving and given up half a day of his time for books that might fetch $40 cash or $45 in credit. And this, to his thinking, was a good piece of business.

"How about a book about Lincoln's law practice?" Michael asked me. "You're interested in laws."

I grimaced.

"Hey, you know that Ginsberg book is still upstairs somewhere," Michael said.

"Hmm," I replied. I was flipping through one of the books Michael had bought, *Savage Night*. It was a reprint of an old crime novel by Jim Thompson. The book's cover heralded Thompson as a writer whose contributions were overlooked in his time—the "Dimestore Dostoyevsky," it called him. The idea of reading Ginsberg bored me. Michael didn't object when I asked if I could take *Savage Night*, which meant it wasn't worth much.

Most of the books Michael kept at home were listed online, but only at prices that would make him willing to part with them. This blurred any line between his collection and his business. He couldn't wind down; he had thousands of books that he could neither sell nor keep. There was no way out.

"Hey, did you see about the rare bookstore that opened up in Pioneer Square?" Michael asked. I had—Michael and I share a login to the *Seattle Times* so we can both read recaps from the Mariners games. "I'm thinking about taking some of my best stuff up there, to see if they'll buy anything."

"You should," I said, hoping to seize on whatever momentum he felt toward thinning his stock. "I have to drive to Seattle next month for work. I can take you. We can reach out to the buyer, maybe get an appointment."

As I spoke, I watched Michael retreat to somewhere I couldn't follow. His eyes went distant, and though he remained in the room with me—approaching eighty, pale and shaggy—he'd already left. "Uh, huh," he said, and stood to follow his thoughts, wherever they'd gone. The thought of selling his books, even just a box or two, threatened to divide the bookseller from the collector, and that division was unbearable.

I moved a stack of old magazines from the middle of the couch, settled into the living room, and began reading *Savage Night*. It was delicious. The book plunged immediately into grotesque crime, but as advertised, Thompson criticized a certain strand of American logic, the kind of self-justification that I encounter in my day job, talking to one stakeholder group or another.

As excited as my parents were to have me over, they both seemed to have quickly forgotten I was there. I looked up from the book only when I noticed the smell of burnt food wafting out from the kitchen. I followed the smell to its source and found Michael at the stove, standing over a plate piled high with scrambled eggs.

"Having eggs?" I asked.

He grunted. "Want some?"

The eggs were golden and crispy on their sides, like hash browns, glistening in the kitchen light. Not the soft, fluffy eggs you might get from a restaurant, but fried hard with a stick of butter that didn't live to tell about it.

"You sharing?" I inquired.

"No," said Michael. "But I'll make you some. You want 'em scrambled?"

I was hungry. But then there was the matter of Michael's kitchen techniques.

We looked each other in the eye.

"Okay," I said.

I looked down at the butter dish, where a fresh stick was ready. I never cooked with butter at home, except maybe for some ghee when I tried my hand at curry. The literature on olive oil was compelling, and while butter could add unctuousness, it was rarely necessary for texture or finish. I liked to cook with precision, to treat ingredients thoughtfully, coaxing out flavor, and composing each dish like a song. Michael hammered everything, eggs included, with a stick of butter.

"It's how I cook 'em," he said.

"I know," I said.

I walked out to the back yard while Michael fired the next round of eggs. Outside, I found my mom putting her weight into a dull, rusted shovel, trying to break the earth of her overwintered garden. Her face was red, and her progress was impeded by the mat of tubers that had taken over, just under the soil.

"Give me a hand, will you?" she said.

I was happy to help, and when I pierced the earth with the old shovel, my suspicions were confirmed. Jerusalem artichokes had come to dominate my mom's garden. Digging them out wouldn't do, either. If you left even a small chunk of the tuber, it would come back strong the next year. Stepping back, I could see that they had taken over not only the garden but the entire yard—so rich had they found the soil for their purposes.

My mom and I knelt down to dig, to remove the tubers at least from a patch of soil big enough that she could plant her garden. There had to be a more systematic solution, I thought.

"Don't you want to just get all of these pulled out?" I asked.

"Just enough to grow some tomatoes," she said.

"What if we got some college kids?" I asked. "Pay them twenty dollars an hour to do the whole yard. Wouldn't it be worth it?"

"Might look nice," she said, holding herself up with one hand and working the ground with the other. "But the weeds give shade to the tomato plants when they're little."

Earlier in my life, I would have judged my mom's resistance to an orderly garden, seeing her stubbornness as flawed thinking. Now I understand that she'd never wanted the kind of garden you might see in a magazine; it wouldn't grow anything good. My mom didn't run on magical thinking—she wasn't foolish enough to spend her life looking for lost books. She had seeded the garden for our family, keeping the weeds back just enough. It reminded me of the equanimity in Kyger's poems. This, not Michael's agitated searching, is what had sustained us.

When the eggs were sufficiently browned, Michael shuffled out from the kitchen, handed me a plate, and retreated into his little office. I followed him back into the house, where I could sit on the couch and listen to him peck away at his keyboard, making entries into an ancient database. With each click and clack, I could hear the wheels of his thought turning. I worked my way through one rubbery bite after another. My eyes wandered from piles of books to old newspapers to half-finished paintings.

My parents had settled some time ago into their own offbeat rhythm of domesticity. Michael's habit of visiting thrift stores around town slowed and then, around the time of his seventy-fifth birthday, had stopped entirely. By then, he'd amassed a formidable collection, piled high in stacks around the floor of his one-story home and creeping up the walls and into the attic, which Michael had increasing difficulty accessing.

I lived near enough that Michael would occasionally call me to climb up to the attic to fetch a book for him. I didn't mind the ladder or the cobwebs, but the futility of his operation drove me nuts. Most of his books sold for $20 to $30, after occupying space in his house for years. While other sellers priced low to move inventory quickly, Michael applied his own assessment of the book's scarcity and condition. He crafted his listings so precisely that their literary quality often exceeded that of the books themselves. In his years online, he'd received essentially no negative reviews.

"Item was well-packaged," raves his top review.

"Superb packaging and condition as described."

"The book, described as 'like new,' was physically perfect in every way. I have never received a book so carefully packaged—I've had new books arrive in envelopes, even padded envelopes, with a dinged corner, but this book was so tightly wrapped in foam and plastic inside the envelope, there was no opportunity for damage. Would definitely buy from this seller again."

But in online sales, there are no repeat customers. And Michael's care came at a cost. He spent fifteen minutes listing each book on a computer so ancient that it took another fifteen minutes just to boot. The books in the house weren't organized alphabetically or by subject, but through an intricate web of associations known only to him. When an order came in—two or three in a good week—he'd spend more on postage than he charged for shipping. Once you factored in his time, Michael valued his labor at a fraction of minimum wage.

Still, each sale thrilled him. For Michael, it was part skill and part good fortune—to find the book, list it perfectly, wait years for a buyer.

How did Michael survive like this? As ever, it was my mom, with her own limited retirement earnings, who sustained him. Michael himself had only his social security supplemental income, since he hadn't paid enough in social security taxes to receive more than the minimum. Because their combined income was only marginally higher than thresholds for public assistance, including food stamps and Medicaid, they still faced Medicare premiums and out-of-pocket costs for prescriptions and care.

With the regular expenses involved in maintaining their aging home, they could meet their obligations for utilities and insurance with a small margin for food and incidentals. Frugality, however, was never a strong suit. Michael wore the same clothes for decades and stretched condiments into meals, but my mom marched to the beat of her impulses, preferring meals out, splurging for the sake of it. This made their financial situation even more precarious than it needed to be.

Though their lives were inextricable from their home, it was unclear that the home and the Whiteaker neighborhood would hold up their end of the bargain. The house itself had recurring issues with electricity, plumbing, and pests, and that's before considering the steps up the front porch. The neighborhood, never a serene place, has been increasingly destabilized by homelessness and addiction, while the opening and closing of brewpubs and distilleries has eroded the sense of community among neighbors.

And then there was the question of how long Michael and Diane would be able to care for themselves. While the delivery economy mitigated some of the challenge of meeting their basic needs, they were the likeliest people on earth to start a fire while attempting to cook a basic meal, which had nothing to do with their age. Where age became a factor was with cognition and mobility; they struggled to hear and understand others, and both had trouble walking. Inevitably, they would have more difficulty bathing and dressing. In the aging and disabilities office, these are referred to as activities of daily living. Not that help would be a bad thing, but when they need it, they will need to spend down what scant savings and assets they have, just to qualify. What would a care provider make of their way of living? Would a stranger be willing to cook their eggs the way they like them, soaked in butter? Would I?

I began visiting more, which meant, for me, finding peace with the home I'd escaped. Every time I walked through the front door, my blood pressure would rise in proportion to the stress caused by their antics. My mom's paint-by-numbers hobby grew more obsessive, taking over half the house, with small buckets of different colors and unwashed brushes tucked into every corner. Michael's books seemed to multiply even as he seldom got out to buy them and became less able to ferry them up to the attic. Michael and Diane went out less, ate more, and groomed themselves about as often as ever, which is to say, seldom.

Michael's gray hair got so shaggy on the sides, around a massive bald top, that he looked like the villain in a children's movie, the kind of character whose avaricious schemes would shock the conscience of a child, like they shocked me when I first met him. Now, I wondered if the avarice and baldness weren't related through some conceit of genetics. Wasn't Michael a kind of real-life villain whose quirks added a touch of comedy to his naked desire for profit? He was perfect for the part, so easily foiled by his own essential flaws.

Done with my eggs, I set my plate in the sink and went to thank Michael. I stood in the doorway to his office, where he hunched over his old computer, deep into the process of describing a $10 book that he'd wrap carefully and ship at a loss. Michael kept the curtains to his office drawn, but the bright overhead light reflected brilliantly from his shiny bald head. The greasy strings of Michael's remaining hair trickled down, almost reaching his shoulders.

"Let me cut it," I said.

"Huh?"

"You want a haircut?" I asked, getting louder. "I'll cut it for you."

Michael grumbled but he didn't object.

"I'll be right back," I said, and I raced back to my own house, where I had a pair of shears that I used to keep myself looking tidy between haircuts. I had no training or experience cutting someone else's hair, but I had shears and scissors, and the urgency to do something to bring order to Michael's aging existence.

When I got back to his house, Michael continued pecking away at his keyboard. He may not have believed I was serious.

"Let's go," I said. I dragged a chair from the house out to the porch so that he wouldn't have to worry about stray clippings getting into his books. Michael came out to the porch, and without saying anything, sat down, facing the street, for all the neighborhood to see. Not that anybody cared.

I held the scissors steady over the balding, bookselling villain, mapping out my plan of attack. He never made any effort to comb his hair; whatever form I left him with that day would be his hairstyle for months, maybe years to come. Maybe forever, since we'd never done this before and there was no reason to think we might do it again.

I began by trimming around his ears. If there was a service I could offer him, having no skills or experience with cutting hair, it would be to remove the hair from the area around his ears so that at least he could hear. And from there, I attempted to cut a kind of shape into the hair around the back of his head, so that, even as the length of each gray strand varied, they all ended in roughly the same place on his neck. Michael started looking less like a bad guy and more like an aging rocker—an improvement, I thought.

Finally, I returned to the front, where I trimmed back the wedges of hair sticking out behind his temples, and then, in a moment of grace or insanity—I'm still not sure—I began trimming the mustache that drooped over his upper lip. I said nothing about this transition from his hair to his face. What was there to say? Instead, I focused on quick, sure strokes with the scissors while he curled his lips inward. I'm not sure if he was more afraid of the scissor blade or of this act, the gentlest thing we'd ever done together—an unplanned trim of the mustache between a crusty old bookseller and an unlikely barber, me, his stepson. I finished with the mustache, gave him a look over, and with that, I was done.

Before anyone had the chance to say or think another word, I swiftly gathered the fallen strands of hair from the porch, discarded them in the trash can, and left Michael sitting out in front of his house.

"All done," I said, already retreating to my car.

"You did good," he said, more to himself than to me.

CHAPTER 17

The Book Business

I was getting ready to settle back into the familiar monotony of my life—work, parenting, searching for books and never finding anything—when something unexpected happened. My phone vibrated with a message from Scott Givens, who had so eluded me that I'd given up on the idea of talking to him. After a quick volley of texts, we agreed to a video call. When he answered, the face looking back at me was cautious but kind. He hadn't meant to miss our meeting, he said, and regretted that he didn't let me know that his plans had changed. Nothing in his eyes suggested that he wasn't interested in talking—only that he was exhausted from what the world had asked of him, or taken from him, already.

"No worries about last Monday," I said. "I'm just glad to talk now."

"Sure," he said. The caution reemerged from behind the kindness, and I could see a wariness in Scott's eyes, maybe wondering why I'd been so insistent.

This was the same question I'd been trying to answer, I realized. What was it that I was looking for from him? What was I trying to find? Even though I had a list of questions that I'd hoped to put to him, I was the one owing an explanation.

"I grew up with Michael Karn," I said. It sounded weird, at least to me, so I elaborated. "He's my stepdad. My dad, really." Then I sensed that I'd said too much, not that I cared what Scott knew about

Michael or me, but it was more than I'd meant to say about the relationship, and it was on a video call with a rare-books dealer who operated, as Gerry put it, on the dark side of the business. What did he care?

I explained that I'd grown up going to book sales and hanging around stores with Michael, whom Scott remembered, and how, after drifting away, I wanted to get back into books. I told him how impressive it was to run a successful bookstore in Albany, and that I'd been fascinated by how different Crooked House had seemed from Browsers'. With this observation, and a few words' distance from my family history, Scott relaxed.

"It's a food chain," Scott said. "Browsers' is intentionally near the bottom. It's above the thrift stores. It's a place where you can come in and get the next James Patterson."

It was surprising to me to hear Browsers' described in less than flattering terms. I'd come to see and love the store through Abe's eyes. But Scott was right. You would not find James Patterson's books at Mother Foucault's.

"Selling books can be lucrative," Scott continued. "Either with quantity or quality. The way that Browsers' works is quantity. What I'm trying to do at Crooked House is quality—fewer books but higher dollars. There are very successful booksellers who sell millions of dollars of books to just a handful of people."

What Scott said was revelatory. I'd never heard a bookseller acknowledge that money could in fact be made. More surprising, Scott had insight into how to do it. It was as though for Scott, bookselling was a business, where for Michael, it was a lifestyle, a way of existing in the world. Same for Gerry and Abe. I wanted to know how Scott had thrived in this world without succumbing to some off-kilter symbiotic relationship with printed matter.

Like Gerry, Scott had moved to Oregon from California, back in the 1990s. Before he ever worked in the business, Scott was an avid reader, haunting used bookstores and sales around Los Angeles. He would read anything. "I would go to library sales and pick up the worst books ever," Scott said. "I kept all my books, but what I was doing then was more hoarding than collecting."

When he arrived in Oregon, Scott had vague plans to go to graduate school—"the path of least resistance"—when he answered an advertisement for a job at a bookstore in downtown Albany. The owner didn't ask Scott about books but instead handed him a Myers-Briggs personality test, on paper, which Scott completed. Whatever the test determined about Scott's personality, it was apparently the right result, and he was hired. The owner handed the operation of the store entirely to Scott, who, new to the business, taught himself everything about how to run a used bookstore. Later, it turned out, the store was being investigated for tax fraud, and the owner had built himself a compound where he stashed his wealth as gold.

Once Scott learned to run the store, he never looked back. He ran it for two years, long enough to get the business off the ground, and since it was at the turn of the twenty-first century, he also managed to launch the store's website. Then he learned enough programming to make a computer database for the store so he could list books online, starting with a small inventory. "There weren't a lot of people selling books, and customers were discovering that you could buy books online," Scott said. "There was a gold rush."

When the store began to make money, he knew that he should be running it for himself. Scott also understood, despite his success selling online, that for the business to be sustainable, he would also need to build a community of readers around a brick-and-mortar store. "Online, people will buy the best copy at the lowest price," Scott said. "At a store, people will come back the next week and buy something else."

Soon, the owner of a paperback shop located inside of an old rambler in Albany, an old grouch named Carl, was looking to retire. "We knew each other, and we liked each other well enough," Scott said. "Well," he added, "we didn't like each other. But we were colleagues." Booksellers, in other words.

Scott and Carl agreed on terms, and then, once Scott had secured financing to buy the shop, Carl backed out of the deal. Another bookstore in Albany, the Book Bin, had announced it was closing, and Carl sniffed an opportunity. He figured his store would be worth more than Scott had agreed to pay. He went back to Scott to see if he could get more. Carl claimed that more money was coming in, and the dealings between them grew tense. Finally, when it was clear that Scott would not pay more than he'd agreed to, Carl went through with the sale on the original terms. It turned out, once Scott got hold of the business, that the Book Bin's closure hadn't changed the habits of paperback mystery readers.

Scott renamed the bookstore from the Albany Book Company to Browsers'. The store's character didn't change much, either, at least at first. It depended on a high volume of transactions involving paperback books, which suited Scott's strengths. "One of my skills is selling stuff cheap," he said. "I learned this at Browsers'. It's what I had to do."

I thought about Abe, how he'd come into this early iteration of Browsers' to buy the first book in his collection, a volume of Rousseau. Abe must have had to look past the shelves of James Patterson and Janet Evanovich to find, in some obscure corner of the store, his foray into French philosophy. But Abe believed, as I had come to, that Browsers' was the best bookstore in the world. Having heard Abe's telling of how he was hired to work at Browsers', I wondered how Scott remembered it.

"I have my own system for job interviews," Scott said. "Probably not something the Bureau of Labor and Industry would approve of. I give a trivia test, but with math. I gear it so that people don't need to know the answer to every question, but to see how people react."

Of everyone who applied for the job, Scott said, "Abe did the absolute worst. He was so bad. He failed utterly." But the point was not to test for knowledge. It was an echo of the Myers-Briggs test he'd been given, to see how an applicant would proceed when they didn't know the answer. "Abe didn't even care," Scott said. "He was like, 'I don't even care.'" It turned out that Abe's unflappability in the face of his uncertainty was the winning quality.

I told Scott how much I'd enjoyed my time around Abe, and the conversation brought us closer. "I wouldn't have wanted anyone else to run Browsers," Scott said. And then, "I was really sad about Browsers' going away," he said.

Finally, I thought, we were approaching the conflict in Scott's story, the tension I sensed everywhere around him, the shape of the thing that got away. "Was it because you wanted to try a different business model in Portland?" I asked, knowing the reasons were more complex.

"Personal stuff," he said. "It had to happen. It was forced upon my life."

And there, I knew, was a place we need not go. I longed to know the history Scott carried with him. But he was right that it was personal, not about books.

When Scott needed to leave the store, Abe said, "Why doesn't someone just give you a little bit of money and keep the store going?"

To which Scott replied, "Yeah, Abe, why don't *you*?"

That conversation happened at ten in the morning, Scott said. Abe took his lunch break at eleven, and by noon he came back and said he'd talked it over with his grandparents, and he was going to buy the store.

Because of other financial obligations, Scott still needed to extract some value from the business, so he arranged to sell the store's better stock to dealers and in sales to the public, which proved to be successful in recouping his investment in the books. The storefront in Albany, and what remained of the depleted stock, was left with Abe on terms that would allow him to grow into the business. If Abe could get the store into the black, he'd pay Scott a nominal amount for the ownership rights.

Scott didn't come out and say he'd seen Abe as anything more than a business partner of sorts, but the terms of the arrangement confirmed as much. Scott had wanted to see Abe carry on something

Scott had built across decades. Nor did Scott require that Abe run Browsers' the same way it had operated.

"He's fooling around with stuff, which is great," Scott said. "It's great to have someone else who's willing to do things differently."

When he left Browsers', Scott left Albany behind and moved up to Portland, where he planned to pursue a new model of bookselling. The way he came in to Crooked House, however, was not only about business. "I originally had a partner who was the founder of Crooked House," Scott told me.

"We would've been a powerhouse," he continued. The model was going to be that Scott and his partner, Rachelle, would buy large collections, and while Scott would sell most of the books cheaply, his specialty, Rachelle would do the research to list and sell high-end stock. Additionally, they would design and print their own catalogs, not just to market their books, but as an expression of their creativity.

Scott's face, as he described the vision, lightened. He'd been in love, I could tell, and he remained in love with their vision for the bookstore, even as it slipped through his grasp. When Scott finished telling me about his ideas for the various catalogs he would make with Rachelle, his eyes returned to his phone, to me. "She died unexpectedly."

It was the most Scott would say about what he had lost.

I thought about Diane di Prima as Scott described, with joy, his vision. It reminded me of di Prima's early endeavors with Amiri Baraka, and also the years-long love affair between them. In her memoir, di Prima describes how her profound love for Baraka powered her poetry, even as Baraka remained married to his first wife, Hettie. This tension simmered in the creative stews of the *Floating Bear*, and it must have been present when Baraka's imprint, Totem Press, published di Prima's first book, the one I'd sought desperately to recover. Like Baraka and di Prima, Scott and Rachelle unlocked each other's creativity. Their connection gave license to whimsy in Scott that was impossible to imagine from any distance, but together, they'd planned and designed catalogs as intricate as most books.

Without his partner, Scott was continuing to work on catalogs, he told me, and the next would involve a collection of books about witches. He specified that these would be books published before the pulp era, when witches in literature were feminized and exploited. I could only imagine the nuanced treatment of witches across literary eras. Scott was working his way through the books to be included in the catalog because he planned to prepare all of the spells he read about in the books. This would require, Scott noted, little glass vials, different kinds of herbs, and eyes of newt.

I wasn't sure, as Scott told me this, precisely why the catalog required him to perform the spells. It was also a different side of Scott than the businessman I'd admired from a distance, this erstwhile witch. The potions, Scott explained, would be kept in a cabinet at the store and could be visited by potential customers.

I wondered if Scott wanted, consciously or not, to bring Rachelle back. I mean, of course he did. Together, they were magic, the result of the spells they'd cast on each other. Still, it was surreal to see Scott, this architect of databases, of matrices of quantity and quality, say earnestly that he planned to mix herbs and eyes of newt inside his own bookstore.

"It seems like being in Portland unlocked something in you," I probed. "Is this about selling books, or is this how you express your creativity?"

Scott's eyes came back to me, and again, were cold. "No dealer is ever supposed to talk about literature as an investment," Scott said. "It crosses a line." And then he crossed it. "I'm always doing numerical or financial analyses of various things. Most books at Crooked House retail from twenty to a hundred dollars. I could sell them easily for one dollar each, or really slowly for a hundred. If I buy three hundred boxes of books, I just need to decide. Usually, the decision is to get rid of the books."

The spell that Rachelle had cast on him was wearing off. Scott was no unicorn, no exception to the profession. He was a bookseller.

"The whole problem is, we have to earn our living," Scott said. "You've got to earn every single dollar. Every day."

This was my cue to leave Scott to his business. I could see the shape of the story—something found, something lost—but there was no way further in. It was not a story for a book. Not something to collect.

I thanked Scott for his time, and we each fumbled to end the call quickly, revealing stray, sideways images of ourselves. Unlike Michael, Scott brought systems-thinking to the book business. It reminded me of how I saw things, but it also helped me understand how little I really knew about this world. I remained an outsider.

CHAPTER 18

Unpacking My Library

I hadn't been to Browsers' in a while when Abe emailed me to say he had an update on *This Kind*. The message came when I was at work in Salem. I left for Albany within minutes. I sped down the highway, oblivious to the public-radio updates about court cases and munitions sales. News of the di Prima was on a different scale.

When I got to Browsers,' Abe waved me in behind the register and together we studied his computer monitor. On it, I saw the book I'd been missing for over two decades: *This Kind of Bird Flies Backward*, published by Totem Press in 1958.

"That's it," I said.

"Yep."

"You found it."

"A listing came up," Abe said. "The seller looks reputable."

"How much?"

"Five hundred, but that's in pounds. I did the math and it's about seven hundred dollars."

"Not bad! I figured it would be two or three times as much."

"It's signed, too," Abe noted.

I leaned in to see the listing more closely. The seller had included several images of the book—its cover and publication page, and the beginning of the title poem, "This Kind of Bird Flies Backward." I thought, *This is it. This could really be it.*

I asked Abe to zoom in, and we both read quietly. The cover was coffee stained and no better than fair condition, but that didn't matter as much to me as having it. Then I noted a detail in the description of the signature. It had been cut from another book and pasted into *This Kind.* It was an amateurish move by a bookseller. Not strictly unethical, but not quite the same as a signed book, either.

Even with those drawbacks, I might still have wanted the book, except for one last, crushing detail: the poem itself. Along with images of the cover, the seller had shared the first page of the poetry. It had been a mistake to include it. What Abe and I read was full of figurative language about love—as essential as bread, as vast as the sea. Worse, the phrase on which everything rested, "This kind of bird flies backward," described not some other way of being in the world, but a literal bird smashing into a windowpane.

I moved out from behind the counter and stood across from it, looking at Abe, who continued to read the description. I didn't want to tell him what I was thinking. We had discussed a 20 percent commission if he found the book, and he had. Worse, he loved di Prima as much as I did, and the search had been every bit as much a joy for him as it was for me. If it were to end like this, where would we go from here?

I knew I had to tell Abe how I felt.

"I think maybe she's not that good," I said.

"What do you mean?"

"As a poet. I don't mean she's bad or anything. But maybe there's a reason she stayed obscure."

"People still want to collect her," Abe said, pleading.

"Oh, sure," I said. "There will always be a market for her books. Anyway, I'm going to pass on this one. I don't like the way the signature is pasted in," I said.

"No worries," Abe said, and he seemed genuinely untroubled. It was Abe's superpower, the reason Scott had first hired him all those years ago and then entrusted him with the store. He was terrible at math, but no matter how complicated things got, how wrong, he was unbothered. I made two resolutions to myself in that instant: first, I was out of the di Prima business. There was no copy, no matter how perfect, that was going to take me back in time or let me keep Michael or anything in this world. Second, every chance I got, I would spend what disposable income I had on used books, from used booksellers. I decided to start right then and there.

"I'm going to shop a little bit," I told Abe, and turned to the fiction section. I found a hardback first edition of a book by Mario Vargas Llosa, who had slipped from the consciousness of collectors as his personal life became weirder. Then I found a hardback collection of Lydia Davis's stories. I asked Abe whether he had a book I'd once heard Gerry describe, by a German writer who wrote thousands of pages of journal entries about living in New York in the 1970s.

"You mean Uwe Johnson?" Abe asked. He showed me the book in a two-volume set, reprinted by the *New York Review of Books.*

"I'll take it," I said. I added to my pile some old Fishtrap anthologies and a bibliography of Ezra Pound poems that were published in periodicals—books I'd noticed at Browsers' months before and couldn't forget. Casting myself as Carter Burden to Abe's Peter Howard, I told him I'd buy anything and everything he could find about the art of D. E. May. And then, as I paid Abe, I recalled what Gary Snyder said about first loves. There will be others, but you won't forget the first. Even if I would never own *This Kind,* I wouldn't forget it, either.

On the car ride home, for the first time, I saw the shape of my own life story. We were still renting an apartment in downtown Eugene, with two small children, while the city was in the throes of the fentanyl crisis. We'd had to call ambulances to respond to overdoses on three different occasions. Our kids hated the apartment because they weren't allowed to run or yell, which were their favorite activities. Lost in my search, I'd been oblivious to all of it.

I'd also been feeling stuck about what to do with Michael and my mom. Never paragons of health, they were aging quickly and struggling with their mobility. Michael still walked, but he shuffled so much that he never quite made it anywhere. My mom had trouble putting her shoes on. I thought, in the way I believed I could solve anything with analysis and planning, that I might be able to craft some arrangement to care for them without also driving myself and my partner crazy.

What I realized on my way home from Browsers', where I'd finally been confronted by the absurdity of my ambitions, was that there was no way I was going to tuck Michael and Diane neatly into a living space within my home, clean up their eccentricities, and send them gracefully into advanced age. They were going to continue to be their messy selves, whether in the Whiteaker or living together with my partner and children. I had wanted to hold on to them, and they had taught me, over the course of our lives, that you can't hold on to anything.

❧

Months later, I decided to stop by the house in the Whiteaker on my way home from work. It was never easy for me at my parents' home because, no matter how hard I tried, I couldn't impose any order on their lives. Growing up, instead of driving around all day to garage sales and cooking unpleasant meals, I had wanted them to make a budget, to do chores, to assign chores to me. Now, I wanted something to be done with the unopened mail and the molding contents of the fridge.

What made me decide to stop that day was a book that Michael had mentioned, that seemed relevant somehow to my decision to let go of di Prima. Something of Ginsberg's, he'd said, up in the attic. I'd remembered the oversized book of photographs, the one we'd bought from David Morrison back in the 1990s. Until Michael mentioned it to David at the book fair, I had all but forgotten about the book. It had been signed, Michael reminded me, not by Ginsberg, but by Gary Snyder. And Snyder hadn't just inscribed the title page as an author would. Instead, he'd written his name carefully next to a photograph of a birthday cake that Diane di Prima had made for his mother. It was another singular book, like *This Kind,* that we'd acquired together—never clearly mine nor his. Unlike *This Kind,* it had survived the churn of Michael's book business. I wanted to find it and keep it safe in my home.

This book was one of a million discordant puzzle pieces that Michael had left around the house. Even if you knew them all as he did, there was no coherent idea to bind them together. With Snyder's signature inside the Ginsberg book, it was rare and perhaps valuable, but in such an unlikely way that only a vanishingly narrow class of beholders might see its worth. Lots of people loved Ginsberg, but for his poetry, not his photographs. Of those, plenty would love Snyder, but then, you had to also be interested in the birthday cake made by an even more obscure poet. Since it wasn't noted in the caption, only a handful of people on earth would know, as Snyder had told me, that the cake was di Prima's work.

The house was quiet and dark, so I finessed the key into the lock on the front door, jiggling the knob until the door popped open and sucked me back inside to the living room, where I was mugged by the smell of old newspapers and wet dog, even though my parents hadn't had a dog since Puppy died in the previous century. In the dim light that filtered into the living room, I saw books stacked against the walls, half-finished paintings stacked among credit card bills stuck to old candy wrappers. Dried paint and balls of chewed pink bubblegum tacked disparate items together.

The living room had the dimensions of a shoe box, not quite big enough for the couch or table or desk or easel or sewing machine that my parents kept there, creating an obstacle course for the rare stranger who visited. The furniture, bought on credit at odd intervals across the last half of their lives, fit no particular style or aesthetic. The bones of the furniture included dark woods with deep reds and greens against walls painted bright yellow, my mom's choice to bring cheer to the room. Every inch that hadn't been claimed by furniture was filled with books that never quite met the destiny that Michael had imagined for them.

This house was not a place where I would choose to spend my time, but because Michael and Diane are my parents, it did more than I care to concede to shape the person I am. I know so well the dull glow of the room's yellow paint that it's the color I see when I close my eyes.

I stepped over a stack of books about railroads, which for support leaned against a half-completed Picasso, its cubes somehow curvy, which was stuck to a *Harper's* magazine from several years ago, a neighbor's address on the label. I bushwhacked my way to the kitchen, where I found the last meal Michael and Diane had eaten before they left the house. On the counter, a block of hardening cheese sat next to a white sleeve of saltines, empty except for crumbs. And next to the wrapper, to complete this feast, was a squeeze bottle of store-brand mustard, one of the few things you can still buy from a grocery store for less than a dollar in these last days of capitalism.

On the other side of the kitchen, in a small passageway between the bathroom and my parents' bedroom, a cord hung from the ceiling, and with a healthy tug, a set of wobbly stairs tumbled down to the floor. I climbed up to the attic where Michael and Diane kept disintegrating blankets, unfinished projects, and several thousand books in unmarked boxes.

Atop one of the boxes was a hand-painted sign that I recalled seeing in some of the various homes we'd made growing up. It read, *This Home is Clean Enough to Be Healthy and Messy Enough to Be Happy*. I was always struck by this informal health code and, in retrospect, by the amount of work done by the second clause. Our houses had been beyond messy, but the logic still applied.

Taking this as a clue, I searched the box of books under the sign, and to my delight, the book of Ginsberg's photographs was there. I do not think my parents could have been organized enough to mark the box in that way, but then, they had a way of making meaning of the world that would lead to the exact confluence of events that placed the sign and the book together. As they were the people who had made me, it followed that I would interpret their clues correctly.

The oversized collection of Ginsberg photographs was majestic to hold in its stiff Brodart, with massive boards. It was heavy, with a stark black cover. As Michael had said, the inscription page was blank, but I could feel some kind of marker tucked into the center of the book. I flipped through photos of the cast of New Yorkers whom Ginsberg had befriended around his village apartment in the 1960s, and opened the book to a photograph of the cake that di Prima had baked for Snyder's mother and, next to the photo, Snyder's shodō-like signature.

Marking the place of this photograph was a stack of photocopies I hadn't seen before. Upon examination, they seemed to be some kind of poem, but not bound as a book. I turned the stack over to reveal the photocopied cover of the book. It was the same cover I had seen hovering over Abe's computer. It was not the original copy of *This Kind* that Michael had sold, but a photocopy of it. I checked the first page, and there I found Diane di Prima's signature, just as it had been in our copy of the book. He had made a photocopy before he shipped it.

What I held in my hands, then, was a facsimile of Michael as much as it was *This Kind*. The photocopied pages were his tenderness and forethought. Michael never demanded attention like a signed first edition. Instead, he was this gesture: a beautiful, forgotten act among teetering boxes of books, worth little to others, worth everything to me.

Michael took temporary possession of the books and bric-a-brac that washed into his life, including me. But then, he also held on to me as a mouthy teenager and through my disaffected twenties. In that way, our bond was no more incidental than Gary Snyder's signature next to a cake baked by Diane di Prima in a book of photographs by Allen Ginsberg. An intrepid human being had allowed his imagination into the folds of the material randomness of the universe, and there a pearl of meaning had formed.

And with this thought, it was time to get *Photographs*—with the copy of *This Kind* stashed inside—out of the attic and the old house. On the way back through the kitchen, I noticed a scrap of paper on the refrigerator, and on it a note to Michael in my mother's blocky, childlike hand:

> MY DEAR,
> LUNCH:
> CHEESE
> CHIPS
> ONE CHOCOLATE
> DO NOT FORGET THE GUACAMOLE
> xx D

That my mother had left these loving instructions for Michael to make her lunch reflected the tenderness I'd always witnessed between them. That her lunch, apparently planned with enough forethought that ingredients had been procured, would include chips and chocolate—and, let's not forget, guacamole—showed the lightness of that love.

Moved by the tender absurdity I saw everywhere in the small house, I retreated out to the porch, felt relief as I locked the door behind me, and got back into my car and drove to the house that my wife and I bought so that our kids would grow up in South Eugene. In the backyard, I found my kids climbing on their grandparents, Papa Mike and Grandma Diane. The fridge was well-stocked with mustard so that we would always be ready to receive them.

I tucked *Photographs* safely away on my shelf, never to be sold.

CHAPTER 19

Loba

Disillusioned by the idea that di Prima's poetry, the beating heart of my quest, simply wasn't any good, I gave myself the sentence I believed worthy of my prejudgment: a solo hike up a steep mountain with di Prima's *Selected Poems 1956–1975* along with her seminal work, *Loba*.

For my penance, I chose the trail from Wallowa Lake up to the summit of the Matterhorn, a mountain that had spent the past century erroneously believed to be the tallest in the Wallowa Mountains. Far from the Willamette Valley, this part of Eastern Oregon feels like a setting for apocrypha. It has lakes that gestate millions of tadpoles, swarms of aggressive insects, and a landscape like the Alps, but hotter, drier, weirder. Surrounded by this strangeness, I was prepared to track down my truth.

I left my family, taking with me a new GPS device that I'd promised to use but would never take out of the box. The risk of getting lost was part of the appeal. I started early in the day to avoid hiking in the crushing heat. It didn't matter. By afternoon I labored under the sun across long zigzags, gaining thousands of feet in altitude, enough that I could feel it in my lungs. When I reached camp at Ice Lake, I felt the kind of deep fatigue that makes it impossible to do anything other than the bare minimum to survive. I inhaled energy bars and took every shortcut possible when I set up camp, producing an REI-branded squalor.

It was here, then, that I finally engaged with di Prima's best known and most exalted work, the *Loba* series. Di Prima wrote *Loba* in the years following her early success as a poet. When she was a younger poet, her work described materially a beatific way of living, with humor and a hint of sensuality. *Loba* was its own creature entirely. Written across decades and published in small chunks—often in small runs, illustrated and printed beautifully—it is the work of the poet confident in her voice and her poetics, unburdened by any expectation about her work.

I set out my camp chair, rested my feet up on a rock, and immersed myself, swatting mosquitoes from my legs between verses. I'd gone in wary of the *Loba* series, again informed by my own prejudice, thinking that it would be about a mystical wolf-woman and that it would not appeal to my sensibilities. The wolf has not been underexamined in literature, from *Little Red Riding Hood* to Aesop's fable about the boy who cried wolf, stories that reveal more about humans than they do about wolves. I'm inclined toward Erica Berry's *Wolfish*—about fear as a cultural construct.

What I found that day on the mountain was something else entirely. Di Prima's *Loba* has no interest in fear whatsoever, nor does it succumb to obvious tropes about desire. The Loba is not some mystical, cartoonish caricature. She is visceral and embodied but made of language rather than literal flesh. She is her own kind of being.

The Loba is a manifestation of feminine strength. The poem, di Prima writes, is for activists such as Emma Goldman, powerhouses such as Billie Holiday and Ma Rainey, and intellectual heavyweights such as di Prima's friend Audre Lorde. The Loba is not unaware of its power to seduce, and occasionally it does, but that is not its purpose or focus. Similarly, it is birthed and gives birth, but again, reproduction is not its object. Instead, the Loba becomes a kind of vessel or holder of images and textures that repeat throughout the poems. The Loba is both flesh and stone, blood and ruby, abalone and marble. The Loba finds and is found in her different forms, but she is never to be possessed.

“NOLO ME TANGERE,” di Prima repeats, reaching back to the Latin she learned at Hunter College High School. *Do not touch me.*

As the sun set over camp, I tucked myself into my tent, my head aching and swimming with desire to understand di Prima. If I'd been seduced, then it was because I'd seduced myself. Di Prima needed no possessor. I fell asleep in the uneasy way that one does after a long hike, cold in the mountain night, waking and drifting off unrestfully. At around one a.m., I woke to find a full moon, beaming like a searchlight down on my tent. I went outside to relieve myself and saw two moons—above and reflected below in the lake. I imagined my face from the moons' perspective, fully illuminated, discovered, found.

That di Prima didn't write any obvious tropes about the moon (I checked the indices of *Selected Poems* and *Loba*) did nothing to temper my conviction that she was with me that night. Startled by this feeling, I struggled to sleep, despite my own exhaustion. There were two of us up there at the lake.

In the morning, everything felt different. The moon was long gone—the Loba had moved on—and the sun crept over the pass to warm me as I made my oatmeal and coffee. At night, I was worn down almost to nothing, broken apart. To be discovered in such a state helped me to find a little bit of myself, to see what it is that holds me together.

Excited, I opened *Selected Poems* and began my relationship with di Prima anew. There, I found the young poet whom I'd been ready to discard after reading only the first page of *This Kind,* but even then, in her early poems, I could also see the poet who would come to write *Loba.* It's true that di Prima traded in tropes of Beat poetry—poverty living and sex and slovenliness. What I discovered as I looked more closely was her keen wit, her awareness of what she was doing. She was always interested in something different, something beyond what we can see and touch, even as she wrote about material experiences.

In di Prima's early poems, her brilliance occasionally broke through. This was true especially in a poem called "The Practice of Magical Evocation," which includes an epigraph from Gary Snyder's *Riprap & Cold Mountain Poems*: "The female is fertile, and discipline (contra naturam) only confuses her." I felt rage in reading Snyder's verse, at his hubris in trying to write something he understood so poorly. Di Prima responded with a kind of poetic grace; she didn't take Snyder to task, but instead allowed his premise ("i am a woman and my poems are woman's: easy to say"), fleshed out his hypothesis ("pelvic architecture functional / assailed inside & out"), and then asked: "what applause?"

> *I create life from words—alchemy—only for you to say that discipline is against my nature. That's what you see, Gary, when you look out at the world?*

Worse, on some level, I'd done the same. I'd created and tended to an idea of di Prima that didn't allow for her depth, for the Loba she was already writing into being, while I dismissed her for the bird and the windowpane.

Agitated, I left camp and began my way up the mountainside from Ice Lake, up to the summit of the Matterhorn. I felt energized, unburdened. I thought about Snyder and his first loves—the mountain, Joanne Kyger. I thought about Michael back when his belly was round, finding *The Uttermost Part of the Earth*. It was not long, in this way, before I came to the top of the Matterhorn and from there, could see the full mountain range on either side and the lake far below. I stayed at the top only briefly, eager to get back down to camp to discover more of the world and myself through di Prima's *Selected Poems*.

On the way down, I pictured Japhy Ryder, Snyder's character in *The Dharma Bums,* bounding down with joyful leaps. Snyder drew his wisdom from the mountains. "I cannot remember things I once read," he wrote from the Sourdough Mountain Lookout, "Drinking cold snow-water from a tin cup / Looking down for miles / Through high still air."

It was a poem about letting go. Snyder loved his mountain so much that he forgot everything and everyone that came before. For me, even at the top of the Matterhorn, it was the opposite. I started to recall everything I'd ever read—verses from Snyder and di Prima, the first chapter of a Kerouac novel I'd read almost thirty years ago. All of it became riprap in the way that Snyder meant it: creek-washed stones cobbled by hand to form a path. It's how I was connected to Abe and Gerry and, ultimately, to Michael. He had never climbed a mountain, had never even gone on a hike, that I can remember. And still, the deeper I looked out into the Wallowas, the more I could sense him there in the gentle dips between peaks, where the mountain goats crossed over.

Snyder had been on to something when he wrote about riprap, but his work was closer to the beginning of the conversation than the end of it. He had passed through New York when di Prima and Amiri Baraka were together, and Baraka thought enough of him to publish *Myths & Texts*. But there was a difference in temperature between the warmth of di Prima's embodied mysticism and Baraka's street-level fierceness and, on the other side of a mountain, Snyder's cool and ordered observations.

In a poem that Baraka dedicated to Snyder, "Way Out West," he describes the hard-won enlightenment you might find in New York, among the junkies on Sheridan Square. It feels almost reproachful of Snyder's ease in nature. Di Prima too saw Snyder's blind spot, his mistaken belief that he could be present, observe, and record the nature of things. Di Prima understood that language doesn't capture; it creates. Far from a well-worn path, language can be wild, powerful. She forged her own idea of nature, the Loba, mystical and unknowable.

I'd understood maybe 10 percent of what I'd read in *Loba*. I knew what all the words meant, but what di Prima gets at, the thing I can barely describe, reminded me of all the pathways I could never see for myself. To devote one's life to literature, for example, or to work at Granary Books in New York. Granary's co-owner, M. C. Kinniburgh—who had edited the occult library catalog that Abe gave me—wrote an entire doctoral thesis about how di Prima and other poets collected and created knowledge. I longed to know first-hand the kind of magick she must have encountered in di Prima's library.

Instead of matching Japhy Ryder's joyous bounds, I took careful, measured steps down from the top of the mountain. I studied each square foot in front of me, watching for loose rocks. In this way, I came to face a mountain goat from no more than ten feet away, the goat heading up the pathway that I descended. We were at an impasse, this goat and me. One of us would have to yield. Observing the goat's horns and its refusal to deviate from our shared path, I stepped aside to let it pass. I noticed that it had a full udder, hinting that it must have kids nearby. Scraggly fur hung from its limbs in dreadlocks. I admired the goat's casual tenacity.

Resuming my descent, I could not distinguish between goat trails and boot trails. There was no riprap to be found at this altitude. It seemed I was now within the web of paths that the goats took from water to shrubs to mountain tops. I crisscrossed wildly down the mountain, inside the goats' brains now, seeing the mountain as they saw it. The descent became too steep if you didn't have a good set of hooves. Finally, I arrived at a patch of snow so steep that even the goats didn't dare. I couldn't figure out how they might descend from there.

As I began to sense that the goat's path had led me to peril, I noticed, in my periphery, the mangy mother goat I'd passed earlier. She stood chewing shrubs at about the same altitude as I, but had taken the path, from where we crossed, up and over to a gentle fold in the mountain, where a stream fed a crease of vegetation. From where I stood, I could see how the goat had traveled from the patch of snow, where she drank, over to the plants she now ate. Step by step, I hiked up and away from the snowbank, across the loose rock, and to the spot where the goat munched blissfully, looking occasionally at me with her weird, diamond eyes.

The goat descended now alongside the stream that gave life to the mountain, taking a gentle zigzag path that I could easily follow. She led me down to a place where the water pooled, showing me a small but impressive lake of clear, icy runoff. From there she left, but I found the boot trail that spurred to the pool from the main trail back down the mountain. I hiked out easily, grateful for all that I didn't understand.

CHAPTER 20

The Book & Paper Fair, Revisited

It was Michael's idea to return to the book fair, this time in the fullest expression of himself—as a bookseller. He asked me first to help with driving and unloading his books. "Of course," I'd said. We would take the campervan that my mom had bought during the pandemic, used now mostly to store books that no longer fit in the house. I offered to get us a hotel room for the two nights we'd be at the fair. Michael seemed happy, or at least as close to happy as he could be, meaning that he had no major complaints. He began preparing months ahead of the sale in June.

The fair had changed in the years since Michael last had a booth, including Scott Givens's new role as the organizer, in place of Rachelle Markley. Michael reached out to Scott to register, and I imagined these two men I knew in conversation speaking tersely, indirectly, about the square footage and tables. Neither would mince words; both had the savvy to endure for decades in the business.

After he'd registered, and as soon as I'd reserved an affordable room at a hotel three blocks from the venue, Michael became preoccupied about the books he would bring. Whenever I had him over for dinner or dropped the kids off to play with their grandparents, he lamented that he didn't have time to get his books ready. What it came down to, as I understood it, was that Michael was struggling to choose which books he wanted to keep for himself and those he was ready to let go of. It raised a question much bigger than the fair itself.

My mom encouraged Michael to pare down his collection—to allow more space in their home, including for my kids to play. It was also his chance, she said, to cash in on some of the equity he'd built up across his career, the same way other folks might draw down a retirement account. As Michael approached eighty, the question of what would become of his books was no less ripe than the question of what would become of him.

In the weeks before the sale, Gerry had come down to help Michael choose books from his collection to sell at the fair and, as was his custom, bought three or four titles, just to be sociable. Michael, however, had complained to me that Gerry was meddling in his affairs, and that Michael knew best what books to bring.

I got the idea that I would set out some books also—from my childhood collection, from my life outside of Oregon, and mostly from the thrift stores and garage sales I'd visited since I came back. I hadn't realized how many books I'd bought during lunchtime walks to the Humane Society Thrift Shop, where I'd found a trove of experimental fiction from the seventies and eighties, along with nearly every book written by Derek Walcott. I'd keep the Walcott for myself. The avant garde novels I could set out at the fair for $5 each, to find their readers.

By the week of the sale, I had ten large boxes full of books that weren't rare or valuable, but that the book-buying public might find interesting. Michael, who had intended to empty his house of some of the thousands of books he'd accumulated, had settled on a similar number of boxes, but the small kind used for shipping odds and ends, each holding five books, maybe ten. After months of ruminating about what to bring, he'd chosen only about a hundred to sell. It felt weird to see my books stacked up next to his in the campervan, like I was taking over.

Anticipating his anxiety on the drive up to Portland, I brought slices of cheese for him to snack on, but he'd brought his own cheese, stored safely in his jacket pocket. He asked repeatedly about the hotel and where we would park the van. He'd been pestering me with parking questions in the days and hours leading up to our departure, and in his obsession, Michael had forgotten his cane, meaning that walking would be more difficult. I'd stick with him, I figured, and we'd manage.

Unlike the year before when we'd attended as visitors, Michael's choice of jacket for this June's fair was his puffy winter coat, grimy and stained from years of heavy use. He wore the jacket from the time I picked him up in Eugene until we arrived in Portland, on a perfect, early-summer day. I wondered if the semaglutide that had slimmed Michael down in recent years had eaten up too much of his natural insulation.

Mercifully, when we arrived, Michael removed his winter coat and changed into the old suit jacket he always wore. The contrast made it seem sharp and new, and Michael was energized by the activity of the booksellers setting up. I began to feel excited as well until, at the registration desk, Michael introduced me as his "helper." The decades away, the family and job and home I'd secured—all of it faded. I'd arrived right back to where I'd started, as Michael's helper.

I chose to embrace my title as my disguise as I reentered the world of bookselling. I guided Michael to our booth along the back row of the fair, where he could rest while I unloaded. Using the same hand truck we'd used decades earlier, I understood that little had changed. Many of the dealers were the same people we'd known then, and they brought the same folding bookshelves that had been used for this purpose. One difference this time, though, was that I had my own boxes to unpack. I did so quickly, setting books out with their spines up on one of the three tables, with a sign that said, *All books $5 or 5/$25*. The idea of selling my reading copies was inspired by my visit to David Abel's Passages booth the year before. It took a few minutes to make my sign and empty my boxes, around the same amount of time it took Michael to unpack just one of his.

Mercifully, Gerry had arrived earlier and set his booth up already, so he came over to help. I observed Gerry's intervention, which Michael had described previously as meddlesome. It was not. Gerry was helping Michael do what was needed, as much as Michael would allow from his peer and friend of more than thirty years. Gerry carefully unpacked boxes and set the books out as he thought Michael would want them. I realized that when Gerry had come down to Eugene in the weeks before the fair, he must have understood then that Michael would need help. It's not easy to know when and how to be useful to someone who is aging. That Gerry sought these opportunities showed deft grace, more than I thought possible from a book scout.

In choosing which books to bring, Michael had not followed Gerry's advice. For example, Michael brought his books about hobos and early labor movements. You could see the thinking—that in Portland, in this particular moment, such topics might appeal—but the problem is that the people most interested in hobos and labor movements were the least likely to spend money on a rare book. Gerry, by contrast, had brought his best art books, modern first editions, and books in translation. Even the latter stood a better chance at this fair.

After he'd helped Michael set his books out, Gerry turned to my offerings and began to shop enthusiastically. He plucked a few volumes from my $5 table, along with some books I'd priced individually—Italo Calvino's *Italian Fables* and a novel by Julio Cortazar, both of which I'd bought from the bookstore inside the Eugene Public Library on the basis of their interesting covers. He got my pristine first edition of Rilke's *Duino Elegies*, which I regretted selling despite the reading copy at home that I'd loved for the last twenty years. By the time he was done shopping, Gerry had found eight or ten books among my offerings and asked me for a price, which was his way of soliciting the dealer's discount. I eyed the books, searching for a fair number. Finally, I chose what I thought was about 60 percent of what I would have charged the public.

When Gerry pulled out his checkbook, I felt a pang of guilt accepting money from someone who'd helped Mike, whom I'd known for so long. But it wouldn't have been right to give the books away, either, so I added another book to Gerry's pile as a sweetener, accepted his check, and folded it into my wallet. When Gerry left, Michael asked how much Gerry had paid, and after I told him, I said I needed to go to Gerry's booth to reciprocate the transaction.

"You know, he always does that. You don't have to buy anything from him," Michael said. I realized that Michael had probably sold books to Gerry unilaterally for years with no compunction to buy anything back. Maybe this dynamic worked for their friendship, but I preferred to show up the way Gerry did, to be the kind of person who helped keep the whole thing going.

I visited Gerry's booth, struggling at first to find something I wanted. He'd brought mostly art books, and while I'm not averse to art, owning a large book by a single artist takes commitment. Among Gerry's prose were several interesting books, including a handsome volume of Baudelaire's *Les Fleurs du Mal*. Like his art books, it was something I could appreciate but didn't feel excited to own. Finally, I spotted a volume of George Saunders's *CivilWarLand in Bad Decline*. I'd been wary of Saunders as sort of a gimmicky writing bro, but one of the stories within that volume, *Bounty*, had stayed with me years after reading it. It had something to say, I thought, about people who'd been forced to live outside, disconnected from society. I'd be glad to own it, and fortunately, the price matched up with what Gerry had spent at my table, though a little less once he'd applied the discount.

With our booths set up and our work done until the fair opened to the public the next morning, we were hungry, and Gerry suggested that we get dinner together. I led us to an Asian fusion spot I'd found nearby, while Michael shuffled behind and Gerry walked next to him, patiently. Gerry was thrilled with the menu at the family-run restaurant, ordered cleverly, and sat down with a cold beer. Michael, meanwhile, read over the menu as though he were savoring the last pages of a great novel, scanning the words again and again to wring meaning from them. Finally, the three of us enjoyed large, hot bowls of noodles and rice, meat and vegetables. We were, all three of us, satisfied.

Michael and I retreated to our hotel and Gerry to his. Michael was relieved that he could see, from our window, the campervan parked in the hotel's lot. I found the hotel itself to be dark and worn down, but Michael loved being there with the heavy drapes and the air-conditioning that sounded like a jet engine. When I turned down the lights, Michael reached for his Walkman and proceeded to listen to cassettes, flipping them over periodically, into the night.

In the morning, I woke with the sun and, to my delight, I found on my phone that a convention for the coffee industry was taking place at the Oregon Convention Center, just blocks away. It was hours before the convention would open, but I dressed for the day and wandered in to check it out.

In a crisp white dress shirt and a suit jacket, I'd dressed formally, having packed from my regular work garb. I must've looked somewhat distinguished, because the coffee people at their booths received me warmly, drawing me into conversation about their offerings. They served me their coffees and gave me samples of beans to take home. They asked me what I was looking for, what kind of business brought me to the fair. Not wanting to disappoint, I explained that I was there as part of a family operation, and that I was always looking to stay on the cutting edge. For an hour that morning, I got to feel like the scion of a successful business venture, to taste the sweet fruits from the top of the tree. It was like reinhabiting one of the characters Michael had created to sell used books to Powell's, but in a weird way, I was also fully myself.

Caffeinated, I returned to find Michael sleeping off a late night with his cassettes, snoring. I cracked the windows, and finally he started to stir, to get ready for our first day back in action together since the 1990s. We arrived at the sale minutes before the doors opened to the public, and in a break room exclusive to booksellers, found an urn with hot coffee and dozens of donuts. I didn't need more coffee, but in helping myself to a maple bar, I'd made my way back into the club—one where I belonged.

The public that had lined up outside began to stream in, eager to see what each booth had brought. This was the same rush I'd gotten the year before, as a customer. The day of this year's fair was also a day of political significance, with a military parade on one side of the country and related protests fanning out to cities like Portland. Some people attended the fair carrying their hand-painted protest signs or wore balaclavas that now hung relaxed around their necks. It occurred to me then that the booksellers I knew were not fervently political people. They might lean in one direction or another, and perhaps that could be inferred by the books they collected. But to engage with the world through books, most of them printed decades or centuries before, was to defy the entire system of contemporary political discourse.

An exception, the dealer across from us had put out a small sign that said, *No Kings*. Looking closer, I recognized the booksellers from my childhood. It was the Prices, Suzanne and Truman, who looked like they'd been around since God was a boy. The Prices had lived out on the old Highway 99W outside of Monmouth, where we had lived for some time when I was growing up. Though we never really knew them, we had seen them at every sale and fair.

I felt drawn to the Prices and wanted to know more about them. I made my way over to their booth and asked about the books they had on display. I didn't tell them that I'd remembered them from my childhood. They wouldn't have remembered me. Instead, I asked them where they sold their books and how they'd gotten into the business. It turns out that they'd been buying and selling books to support the school Suzanne had run from their home. If I wanted to know more about their experiences, Truman interjected, I could buy his memoir. That such a thing existed thrilled me, and I bought it immediately, before we'd finished our conversation. I thanked them for the book. I wanted to thank them for the lifetime they'd given to the trade.

David Morrison, whose politics would not have mapped neatly onto the day's discourse, was nowhere to be found at this year's sale. Like Gerry, he was someone who I took for granted would always be wherever Michael went. I wondered whether the cell-phone signals had finally gotten to David. I hoped he'd just decided to take a year off from the fair, but I worried, knowing how hard it could be for an old bookseller to come back.

Back at our booth, which was called Balcony Books, the name Michael had used at his last store in Eugene, I found that my books had made up most of our sales. Younger buyers picked up my paperbacks of James Baldwin and Alan Watts, even my first copy of *Nova Express.* Any regret I might've felt about selling those books I'd once cherished was overwhelmed by the joy at seeing them in the hands of people who looked forward to reading them. For the first time, I could almost understand the appeal of selling books.

Michael wasn't selling many books, but while I had been talking with the Prices, one of the principals of Burnside Rare Books had stopped by our booth and had agreed to buy Michael's most expensive book, a hardback first edition of John Steinbeck's *East of Eden.* It was a huge sale for Michael, justifying the time and resources we'd invested in the fair. Not that it made the event profitable, but it meant, at least, that he wouldn't lose money.

The way the dealers from Burnside bought books matched their tony catalogs. They went from booth to booth, choosing the best books and promising to come back later with a check. They were at the top of the food chain, as Scott had described it. They weren't here to sell books, but to buy them to be resold eventually, to customers the likes of which Michael would never know. If the Burnside operation felt exclusive, well, it was. But it also served an important role: For many dealers, Michael included, it made the business viable.

Once I let down my guard, I found the people from Burnside to be compelling also. The well-dressed clerk who had, to my annoyance, pointed out the signed first editions the year before approached as Gerry and I were chatting. She introduced herself to me and greeted Gerry warmly.

"We all love Gerry," she said, and I realized that my orientation to this world couldn't have been so different from hers, even if her boots cost more than all the books I'd sell that day. Gerry told me that she worked on catalogs, as Gerry had done in Berkeley, and Diane di Prima in New York—as I had tried once, too.

I watched our booth while Michael caught up with Gerry. He asked about Gerry's room at the Motel 6—"Okay," Gerry said—and then he proceeded to brag about the top-notch hotel I'd secured for us, and above all, the convenient parking it offered. Gerry nodded graciously as Michael made sure that he and anyone within earshot knew who had the better hotel. I turned my attention to the people who shopped among our books.

It thrilled me when the proprietor of Mother Foucault's shopped among my books and found a volume of Seamus Heaney's poetry that was no doubt underpriced. To know that a book of mine would join his esoteric collection was worth it. David Abel himself visited my table and found a stack of obscure poems that hadn't interested me in the slightest until he picked them up, at which point I wanted to recapture everything he bought. I made a mental note of one particular book, *On Being Blue* by William Gass, to look up later. After the sale, I ordered the book online, paying more for it than David had paid for the stack he bought from me.

When lunchtime came, the dealers returned to the breakroom for trays of sandwich wraps and vegetables with ranch dressing. It was not a fancy lunch or even a particularly good one, but something about having access to the food that sustained the rest of the dealers thrilled me. Michael wasn't disappointed, either. We took turns eating our lunch, and when it was my turn, I lurked among the other dealers, who discussed their business dealings from the last year. I overheard one dealer describing his trip to sell books in

England and Scotland, and the sheer joy he'd found searching for books abroad. I watched another dealer wrestle with the coffee urn to extract the last few drops of the nectar he needed to sustain himself that day. I loved feeling like one of them.

With the money I'd made from my sales, minus what I'd paid to Gerry, I let myself look around to see if there was anything I wanted to add to my own collection. At David Abel's booth, I found some of the same titles that I'd set out at my booth. This made me more keen on my own books, including volumes by a poet named David Wagoner, three of which I subsequently plucked from my table and set aside to keep in my collection. As I listened to David chatting with other customers, I realized that I liked his voice, his way of being in this world. I decided that next time I was at Passages, I would buy a book of his poetry.

At the very end of my loop through the fair, I came across a booth consisting of several stacks of books set out in deliberate piles by booksellers calling themselves the Bottomfeeders Collective. It was unlike anything I'd seen, and it matched my imagination of the blanket that Michael would set out in his early days at Fairhaven College. While not organized around any specific interest, there was a kind of thematic coherence to the books, and each time I picked one up, it made me want another. I bought an early book by David Barthelme, a forgotten short-story writer whose experimental style hinted at Saunders; and two collections of stories by Jorge Luis Borges, in Spanish, with one discounted because the pages were uncut. To collect, it is not required to read the book.

I was relieved that I didn't see any of di Prima's books at the sale. I'd have been forced to revisit the fragile peace I'd found. I did, however, come across another pristine volume of the *Mazamas* magazine in which Snyder had published his first essay about the mountain and first love. Like the year before, it was within a glass case, but this year, I took the brave step of asking to see it. I read the first few lines of Snyder's essay—about the mountains he'd never forget. Instinct took over and, flush with cash, I bought it, a recapitulation to my own first love. Returning sheepishly to our booth, I slipped past Michael and hid it with *CivilWarLand*.

After Michael sold his Steinbeck, his first day was made more triumphant when his daughter, who had found Michael through an ancestry search, visited us at the fair. Kim is a kind and gentle soul, with Michael's best qualities, including his blue eyes. I was glad to let her sit with Michael so that I could wander the fair. When the day's business was done, we all went out for sandwiches together, celebrating our successes with a French dip and its salty cup of au jus.

The next morning, with a full day of bookselling, packing up, and the drive back to Eugene ahead of us, I decided to get us started by walking across the bridge to downtown Portland to bring back croissants. This time, Michael had not slept in, and when I checked my phone, I had several frantic messages asking where I was, hours before the fair opened. I found Michael sitting on the edge of his bed staring warily, his blue eyes catching the light from the window of the motel. I offered him the croissant, which had come from a well-recommended bakery.

"Thanks," Michael said. "But it's a little bit crummy."

We packed up, checked out, and returned to the sale. A steady stream of business continued and, to my delight, a couple of my colleagues who live in Portland visited our booth. As I introduced them to Michael, I felt the tension of two worlds coming together, but also relief and excitement that I could be myself, one person with a foot in each world. One friend bought a book of poetry from Gerry priced at the exact difference between what Gerry paid for my books and what I had paid for his, meaning that, at least for a moment on a Sunday in June, the universe was in harmony.

Toward the end of the day, Abe visited the fair from Albany and stopped at my booth. I was excited to see my friend. When he bought a handful of books from me, we joked that it wasn't from a sense of any obligation, a nod to Gerry's mentorship of both of us. As the fair ended, with my heart full, I loaded the van. Too quickly, we were back on the road, heading south on I-5.

"What was your favorite thing that happened?" I asked Michael. I thought about what it might mean to him, after three decades, that I would come back to his world, to help with accommodations, and even to sell some books of my own.

"This," Michael said, unfolding his wallet and holding out his check from Burnside Rare Books. Michael gave me a sly smile. I knew how he felt, even if he didn't say it.

❧

The following weekend, all I could think to do was to call Michael to see what he was up to, and all he could think to do was look for books. He reminded me about the junk seller down in Cottage Grove who had bought an old scout's collection and was selling it off in small chunks. We agreed to make the thirty-minute drive together. I decided to bring along my little boys, Aaron and Ben, who were then four and six years old and who loved books. That they'd started collecting baseball cards was a sign that they might be ready for this kind of mission. What I had learned in the last year was enough for me to let go of the trepidation I'd had about passing on the precarious trade.

We didn't tell the kids where we were going, or that we intended to shop for books to resell. How would you explain it to a child? Instead, when we arrived, the four of us poured out of the car and into the junk shop, led by instinct. I found a copy of *The Recognitions* by William Gaddis. It was one of the thousand-page books assigned by Abe to his reading club at Browsers'. I would be happy to keep a copy on my shelf—never, I hoped, to read.

Michael found a handful of crisp paperback copies of Raymond Carver's books, all of which we'd both read and owned already. He'd buy them anyway, maybe to resell. Ben found a coffee-table book about the Brooklyn Dodgers full of black-and-white photos of what he claimed was his favorite team. As he followed me to the fiction section to inspect Michael's Carvers, Ben held tightly to his book about a baseball team that had ceased to exist—at least in its original form—halfway through the twentieth century.

We stopped at a deli in Cottage Grove, and Michael and I ate sandwiches while the boys looked through their books.

"Want to go to the book fair again next year?" I asked.

"Maybe next year we don't get a booth to save money," Michael said. "I'll bring in a few books for Burnside to look at."

"Your plan is to smuggle books into the book fair?" I said, feigning surprise. "What about getting rid of all your books?"

"Call Scott and get a booth next year," he said. "You can take them."

Author's Note

Thanks to the booksellers—Abe Richmond, Gerry Rouff, and of course, Michael Karn—who let me into their world. If you like used bookstores, be sure to buy something.

Standard memoir disclaimers apply to this book also. Dialogue is reconstructed from memory, and events are described as precisely as possible, subject to the author's fallible memory.

Thanks to everyone who read early drafts and helped me figure out how to tell the story: Nancy Austin, Donna Bunten, Melisa Bush, Dana Dart-McLean, Diane Dietz, Matt Goodwin, Aleria Jensen, Michael Karn, Perrin Kerns, Elana Kirschner, Kris Kolta, Beth McMurray, Tami Meek, Ursula Villarreal-Moura, David Zaworski. Thanks especially to Greg Bocquet for reading three times, and to Carrie Coates who read twice (in the precious hours when the kids were asleep). This book was made by the time you gave.

Thanks to Kim Hogeland and Oregon State University Press for turning this into a real book, and to Nick Neely for his indispensable feedback during the review process. Thanks to the community at Fishtrap for showing me how it's done. Thanks to everyone who gave me a place to write: Melisa and Bill Bush (we miss you, Bill), Lizzy Coates, and the Olseth Family Foundation.

Thanks especially to Carrie and to my rare first editions, Ben and Aaron, whom I will never let go of.

Books Referenced

Diane di Prima's memoir, *Recollections of My Life as a Woman: The New York Years* (New York: Viking, 2001) provided context that was crucial to telling this story. Books and texts are listed under the chapters where they are quoted from or centrally discussed.

THE ROSE CITY BOOK & PAPER FAIR

A Convergence of Birds: Original Fiction and Poetry Inspired by the Work of Joseph Cornell. Ed. Jonathan Safran Foer. New York: D. A. P., 2001.

di Prima, Diane, and LeRoi Jones, eds. *The Floating Bear: A Newsletter, nos. 1–37, 1961–1969.* La Jolla, CA: Laurence McGilvery, 1973.

Ginsberg, Allen. *Photographs.* Altadena, CA: Twelvetrees Press, 1990.

Snyder, Gary. "The Youngsteigers." *Mazama* 29, no. 13 (December 1947).

Stafford, Kim. *Having Everything Right: Essays of Place.* Lewiston, ID: Confluence Press, 1986.

THE APPRENTICE

Angell, Roger. *The Summer Game.* New York: Viking Press, 1972.

Bouton, Jim. *Ball Four.* New York: World Publishing, 1970.

SANDWICH DAYS

Bridges, E. Lucas. *Uttermost Part of the Earth.* London: Hodder and Stoughton, 1948.

THIS KIND OF BIRD FLIES BACKWARD

Burroughs, William S. *Naked Lunch*. Paris: Olympia Press, 1959.

Burroughs, William S. *The Ticket That Exploded*. Paris: Olympia Press, 1962.

Burroughs, William S. *Nova Express*. New York: Grove Press, 1964.

Burroughs, William S. *The Wild Boys*. New York: Grove Press, 1971.

di Prima, Diane. *This Kind of Bird Flies Backward*. New York: Totem Press, 1958.

di Prima, Diane. *Dinners and Nightmares*. New York: Corinth Books, 1961.

di Prima, Diane. *Memoirs of a Beatnik*. New York: Olympia Press, 1969.

di Prima, Diane. *Revolutionary Letters*. San Francisco: City Lights Books, 1971.

di Prima, Diane. *Loba as Eve*, Parts I and II. Limited editions, 1970s.

di Prima, Diane. *Recollections of My Life as a Woman: The New York Years*. New York: Viking, 2001.

Ginsberg, Allen. *Photographs*. Altadena, CA: Twelvetrees Press, 1990.

Snyder, Gary. "The Youngsteigers." *Mazama* 29, no. 13 (December 1947).

Snyder, Gary. *Myths and Texts*. New York: Totem Press, 1960.

BUYER BEWARE

di Prima, Diane. *This Kind of Bird Flies Backward*. New York: Totem Press, 1958.

MICHAEL'S BOOKS

di Prima, Diane. *This Kind of Bird Flies Backward*. New York: Totem Press, 1958.

NONFICTION

Goodman, Gary. *The Last Bookseller: A Life in the Rare Book Trade*. Minneapolis: University of Minnesota Press, 2021.

O'Neil, Shauna and Ariel Low. "Older Oregonians: Mapping Oregon's Older Adult Population Now Through 2050." Legislative Policy and Research Office, Oregon State Legislature, October 27, 2023. Data from Portland State University Population Research Center, reprinted with permission.

MYTHS & TEXTS

di Prima, Diane. *This Kind of Bird Flies Backward.* New York: Totem Press, 1958.

Snyder, Gary. *Myths and Texts.* New York: Totem Press, 1960.

WHAT KYGER KNEW

Kyger, Joanne. *The Tapestry and the Web.* San Francisco: Four Seasons Foundation, 1965.

Kyger, Joanne. *Going On: Selected Poems 1958–1980.* New York: Dutton, 1983.

Kyger, Joanne. *Just Space: Poems 1979–1989.* Santa Rosa, CA: Black Sparrow Press, 1991.

Kyger, Joanne. *Again: Poems 1989–2000.* Albuquerque, NM: La Alameda Press, 2001.

Kyger, Joanne. *As Ever: Selected Poems.* New York: Penguin, 2002.

Kyger, Joanne. *About Now: Collected Poems.* Orono, ME: National Poetry Foundation, 2007.

Kyger, Joanne. *On Time: Poems 2005–2014.* San Francisco: City Lights, 2015.

Mount Eerie. "Belief." Lost Wisdom pt. 2. P. W. Elverum & Sun, 2019 (quoting Kyger, "Desecheo Notebook").

BROWSERS' BOOKS

di Prima, Diane. *This Kind of Bird Flies Backward.* New York: Totem Press, 1958.

Wallace, David Foster. *Infinite Jest.* Boston: Little, Brown, 1996.

SERENDIPITY

Basbanes, Nicholas A. *A Gentle Madness: Bibliophiles, Bibliomanes, and the Eternal Passion for Books.* New York: Henry Holt, 1995.

Howard, Peter. *Serendipity Books Catalogue 16: Modern Literature.* Berkeley: Serendipity Books, [undated].

PASSAGES

di Prima, Diane, and LeRoi Jones, eds. *The Floating Bear: A Newsletter*, nos. 1–37. 1961–1969. La Jolla, CA: Laurence McGilvery, 1973.

Gaddis, William. *The Recognitions*. New York: Harcourt, Brace, 1955.

May, D. E. Inland Waterways, Correspondence. 2017.

Oliver, Mary. *No Voyage and Other Poems*. London: Dent, 1963; New York: Houghton Mifflin, 1965.

FRIENDSHIP

Kinniburgh, Mary Catherine. *A Catalog of the Diane di Prima Occult Library*. New York: TKS Books, 2023.

CROOKED HOUSE

Bersani, Leo. *Baudelaire and Freud*. Berkeley: University of California Press, 1977.

Gantos, Jack. *Rotten Ralph*. Illustrated by Nicole Rubel. Boston: Houghton Mifflin, 1976.

le Carré, John. *Silverview*. New York: Viking, 2021.

Maynard, Joe, and Barry Miles. *William S. Burroughs: A Bibliography 1953–73*. Charlottesville: University Press of Virginia, 1978.

Snyder, Gary. *Riprap and Cold Mountain Poems*. San Francisco: Four Seasons Foundation, 1965.

Stafford, William. *The Way It Is: New and Selected Poems*. Minneapolis: Graywolf Press, 1998.

Stegner, Wallace. *The Writer in America*. Tokyo: Hokuseido Press, 1952.

MOTHER FOUCAULT'S

Benjamin, Walter. "Unpacking My Library: A Talk about Book Collecting." *Illuminations*. Edited by Hannah Arendt, translated by Harry Zohn. New York: Schocken Books, 1969, pp. 59–67.

PARTIAL ECLIPSE

Thompson, Jim. *Savage Night*. New York: Lion Books, 1953.

UNPACKING MY LIBRARY

di Prima, Diane. *This Kind of Bird Flies Backward* [photocopy]. Original: New York: Totem Press, 1958. Photocopied by Michael Karn, ca. 2002.

Ginsberg, Allen. *Photographs*. Altadena, CA: Twelvetrees Press, 1990.

LOBA

di Prima, Diane. *Selected Poems 1956–1975*. Plainfield, VT: North Atlantic Books, 1975.

di Prima, Diane. *Loba*. Berkeley: Wingbow Press, 1978.

Jones, LeRoi. "Way Out West." *The Dead Lecturer*. New York: Grove Press, 1964.

Kerouac, Jack. *The Dharma Bums*. New York: Viking Press, 1958.

Kinniburgh, Mary Catherine. *Wild Intelligence*. Amherst: University of Massachusetts Press, 2022.

Snyder, Gary. "Mid-August at Sourdough Mountain Lookout." R*iprap and Cold Mountain Poems*. San Francisco: Four Seasons Foundation, 1965.

THE BOOK & PAPER FAIR, REVISITED

Gass, William H. *On Being Blue: A Philosophical Inquiry*. Boston: David R. Godine, 1976.

Price, Truman. *Canora: Notes From an Old-Time Fiddler*. Self-published, 2017.

Rilke, Rainer Maria. *The Selected Poetry of Rainer Maria Rilke*. Edited and translated by Stephen Mitchell. New York: Vintage International, 1989.

Saunders, George. *CivilWarLand in Bad Decline*. New York: Random House, 1996.

Snyder, Gary. "The Youngsteigers." *Mazama* 29, no. 13 (December 1947).